FLIPPING PROPERTIES

Second Edition

Generate Instant Cash Profits in Real Estate

William Bronchick, Esq.
Robert Dahlstrom

KAPLAN PUBLISHING

This publication is designed to provide accurate and authoritative information in regard to the subject matter covered. It is sold with the understanding that the publisher is not engaged in rendering legal, accounting, or other professional service. If legal advice or other expert assistance is required, the services of a competent professional should be sought.

President, Kaplan Publishing: Roy Lipner
Vice President and Publisher: Maureen McMahon
Acquisitions Editor: Victoria Smith
Senior Managing Editor: Jack Kiburz
Typesetter: Elizabeth Pitts
Cover Designer: Scott Rattray, Rattray Design

Published by Kaplan Publishing,
a division of Kaplan, Inc.

Printed in the United States of America

07 08 09 10 9 8 7 6 5 4

Library of Congress Cataloging-in-Publication Data

Bronchick, William.
   Flipping properties : generate instant cash profits in real estate / William Bronchick and Robert Dahlstrom.—2nd ed.
      p. cm.
   Includes bibliographical references and index.
   ISBN-13: 978-1-4195-3551-2
   ISBN-10: 1-4195-3551-X
   1. Real estate investment. 2. House buying. 3. House selling. 4. Real estate business. I. Dahlstrom, Robert, 1962– II. Title.
   HD1382.5.B755 2006
   332.63'24—dc22

                                     2006004137

We have been blessed by the support of many people in our lives. We are thankful to live in a country where we are free to pursue our dreams, and we hope this book helps others to achieve their own success.

Real estate has probably made more millionaires than any other financial vehicle. A full-time or part-time venture into real estate investing offers many financial and personal rewards, including cash flow, security, and long-term wealth. There are many ways to profit in real estate. The question is, which method is right for you? A wise investor eventually develops skills and resources to apply with each method.

TRADITIONAL APPROACH TO REAL ESTATE INVESTING

The traditional concept of real estate investment requires one to invest money, then wait for something to happen. Typically, people buy real estate for income and appreciation. They expect that, after 30 years or so, their mortgages will be paid off, and they will receive a generous cash flow for their retirement years. These assumptions are generally correct, and many people have become wealthy by owning rental real estate. Rental properties continue to be an excellent vehicle for creating long-term wealth and income for retirement. However, acquiring and managing rental properties requires cash for down payments, credit to obtain financing, and time to deal with tenants. We do not discourage owning rental properties; rather, we suggest that you get some experience and working capital before venturing into rentals.

THE SPECULATOR'S APPROACH

Some investors are speculators; that is, they buy property or invest in development projects they expect will go up in value, creating a good return on the capital invested. This increase in value depends largely on outside factors, such as rezoning, surrounding developments, and market inflation. Although many people have made millions of dollars on real estate speculations, just as many have gone bankrupt. Thus, speculation is a large gamble and not well suited for inexperienced investors.

THE "NOTHING-DOWN" APPROACH

"Nothing down" is another concept in the real estate world. Many beginning investors are lured to real estate by the late-night television gurus showcasing their millionaire students who bought real estate with no money. Beware: Many of these people are paid actors, and some are just plain lucky. Investing no money in real estate usually means that most of the funds for the acquisition price are borrowed. Highly leveraged real estate purchases can often lead to negative cash flow when vacancies arise or when repairs or even routine maintenance is required. The people you don't see are the ones who bought properties with no money down and who have no cash reserves for the difficult times. Case in point: Tens of thousands of highly leveraged investors lost all their properties in the real estate crash of the late 1980s.

Not all gurus are frauds, and buying real estate with nothing down is not always a bad idea. Just be wary of exaggerated claims that real estate investing is a fast or easy way to get rich. In real estate, a general rule is you can get a good price or good terms, but usually not both.

THE WAY THINGS ARE IN THE REAL WORLD

The reality is that real estate is like any other business. You don't get rich overnight; it takes hard work and time to accumulate wealth. In fact, most start-up companies actually lose money their first year or two. The companies that survive past the first few years, however, often become profitable and continue to grow. While you may make money right away in your real estate business, you may not see a substantial profit for several years.

Because most businesses fail in the early years from lack of cash flow, we recommend you generate working capital before you buy properties that are keepers. Certainly, you can buy properties with little or no money down, but you will need cash reserves to get you through the difficult times that every investor encounters. While a comfortable retirement is a worthy goal for all real estate investors, we all have to pay our bills along the way; equity will not feed you and your family. A sound businessperson focuses first on generating cash flow, then on growing the business. The real estate business is no exception.

WHAT TO EXPECT FROM THIS BOOK

This book will teach you, step by step, how to generate cash by buying and quickly reselling (flipping) properties. In Chapter 1, you will be introduced to the basic concepts of flipping properties. Chapter 2 covers the necessary mechanics of real estate transactions. In Chapters 3, 4, and 5, you will learn how to locate, analyze, and negotiate the purchase of a bargain property. In the later chapters, you will learn how to renovate, finance, and sell your properties for healthy cash profits in any real estate market. In addition, we will review the appropriate legal and tax issues and give you a game plan for launching a successful investment career. In the appendixes, you will find valuable legal forms, contracts, step-by-step checklists, and sample advertising and marketing materials.

Are you a beginner looking to generate some immediate cash? Perhaps you are working full-time and are trying to obtain additional income or find a new career. Possibly you are up to your ears in debt and see no way of paying off your credit cards. Regardless of your personal situation, this book will help you earn the cash you need to accomplish your goals.

WHAT'S NEW ABOUT THIS BOOK?

Since this book was first published in 2001, millions of people have been introduced to the concept of fixing houses for resale through cable television shows, infomercials, and other sources. Many people with little or no investing experience are applying techniques used by investors to add value to their houses for resale purposes. Others are turning to flipping as a way to earn extra income or as a new career. The sound business practices set forth in this book are timeless. However, this new edition includes discussions of the latest investment trends and developments. Being armed with this information is sure to increase any real estate investor's chances for success.

Based on feedback from readers and our own experiences, we've added new concepts throughout the book, added to the appendixes, and introduced several chapters of all-new material. Even if you have previously read *Flipping Properties,* read through the complete text of this updated edition. Then prepare to jumpstart your income.

1

THE CONCEPT OF FLIPPING PROPERTIES

Real estate, like any other commodity, is bought and sold every day of the week. Many people become real estate agents because they know a small piece of a large pie means big bucks. Agents help facilitate a sale by finding a willing buyer for a willing seller, earning a commission of 4 to 7 percent of the sales price for making the deal happen.

Getting a real estate license is relatively simple, and selling real estate is a lucrative field for many people. As you might expect, however, strong competition exists among agents. The successful agents work long, hard hours. In fact, most agents are on call weekends and nights with their cell phones glued to their ears. Furthermore, real estate agents are required to take continuing education classes and follow strict guidelines set forth by government agencies. There are better ways for an entrepreneur to make a living!

THE FLIPPER

Investors who flip houses accomplish the same basic task that real estate agents accomplish. Specifically, the flipper investor buys real estate with the intention of immediately reselling for profit. As a flipper, the investor buys properties at substantially less than the going or retail rate. The flipper acts as both principal and middleman, buying at one price and reselling at a higher price.

If a deal is marginal (with not much profit in it) and the investor adds no value to the property, the flipper's profit is commensurate with that of a real estate agent. Unlike an agent, however, the flipper may have only a few hours of time tied up in the deal. Furthermore, the flipper's upside profit potential is much higher than an agent's commission, because an occasional bargain purchase can bring a tremendous return. The flipper neither needs a license to practice nor works under the watchful eye of a government agency. The flipper benefits from low overhead and flexible work hours and doesn't have to drive a Mercedes to be taken seriously. (But a successful flipper can certainly afford one!)

DIFFERENT TYPES OF FLIPPERS

There are three types of flipper investors, usually based on experience:

1. Scout
2. Dealer
3. Retailer

The Scout

Scouts are information gatherers. They find potential deals and sell the information to other investors, much like a bird dog that brings ducks back to its master. (In fact, scouts are sometimes called bird dogs.) Many people get started as a scout for other investors because looking for distressed properties does not require any cash or prior knowledge.

What is a Distressed Property?

A distressed property is one that creates emotional or financial distress for its owner. Distress may be caused by the owner's financial problems or the fact that the property is in need of repair. Either way, the owner is motivated to sell the property at a discounted price.

Scouts find a property for sale, gather the necessary information, and then provide this information to investors for a fee. The fee varies, depending on the price of the property and the profit potential. Scouts can expect to make $500 to $1,000 each time they provide information that leads to a purchase by another investor.

The scout should gather as much information about a property as possible, such as

- the complete address of the property,
- the owner's name and telephone number,
- a photograph of the house,
- information about the owner's asking price and loan balance and whether the payments are current,
- liens on the property,
- summary of information about the condition of the property, and
- information about the owner's motivation to sell (e.g., foreclosure, needs repairs, divorce, etc.)

The scout may speak to the owner directly or gather information from public records or other means. The scout's most important job is to identify a property owner who is motivated to sell at

> ### Will Someone Steal the Deal?
>
> The beginning scout may be wary of providing too much information to investors for fear of someone stealing the deal. This rarely happens; experienced investors know the unhappy scout will not bring any future deals their way.

a discounted price. Keep in mind that the owner of a house in need of repair is not necessarily motivated to sell. Many property owners can afford to fix a property or let it sit vacant for months or even years. The motivated seller does not have the means or the will to handle the problems presented by the property.

For example, a scout drives by a boarded-up house with an overgrown lawn and old newspapers piled up on the stoop. The scout speaks with a neighbor and learns the name and telephone number of the owner. The scout then talks with the owner and discovers the property is in foreclosure and the owner does not have the means to repair the property or make the mortgage payments. The owner is open to all suggestions, but the scout has neither the means nor the experience to solve the owner's problem. The scout sells the information about the property and its owner to another investor.

The Dealer

Dealers, like scouts, locate deals for other investors. They find a bargain property and sign a purchase contract with the owner. Dealers then can close on the property and sell it outright, or just sell their contracts to another investor. (See Chapter 2.) Dealers are providing more than just information; they are controlling the property with a binding purchase contract. Dealers often put up earnest money to secure the deal, so they assume more risk than the scout does. Because dealers control the property with a purchase contract, they have greater profit potential than the scout does.

Dealers often resell the property in its "as is" condition. Dealers, however, can sometimes increase their profits by cleaning up their properties. (This approach, known as a quasi-rehab, is discussed in Chapter 11.) In fact, a simple cleanup job may increase the dealer's profit by several thousand dollars. While most investors can see past the mess, a spruced-up property is psychologically more appealing to any buyer, even an experienced one. The dealer does not need to perform repairs or upgrades but simply cleans up the appearance of the property by removing junk and debris, cleaning windows, and cutting the lawn. This type of labor can be hired out for a few hundred dollars. Don't pay a premium price for a professional cleaning crew that advertises with a full-page ad in the phone book. Check the classified ads of your newspapers or the local *Pennysaver* for a mom-and-pop operation with a pickup truck, a broom, some trash bags, and an old lawn mower.

Dealers can flip as many deals as they can find. On a full-time basis, a dealer can make well over $20,000 a month without ever fixing a property or dealing with a tenant. On a part-time basis, a dealer could easily make an extra $5,000 a month flipping a property or two. The lifestyle of dealers is that of true entrepreneurs; they can work as much or as little as they like with no boss, no employees, and the freedom to do as they please.

The Retailer

Retailers usually buy a property from a dealer or with the assistance of a real estate agent or scout. The retailer's goal is to fix up the property and sell it for full retail price to an owner-occupant. Compared to other flippers, the retailer puts up the most money, takes the most risk, and stands to make the largest profit on each deal. However, it may take the retailer months to realize a profit, unlike the scout and dealer who make their money in a matter of days or weeks.

Before someone can become a successful retailer, that person must have a working knowledge of how to renovate a house, particularly the cost of doing so. A good dealer also should have a rough idea of the cost of repairs to buy properties at the right price and resell them to the retailer. A dealer who pays too much for a property will have a difficult time reselling it to a retailer. Likewise, the retailer who pays too much will have a difficult time making a profit upon resale to an owner-occupant.

It may make sense for the newer investor to work with a more experienced partner. This arrangement allows the new investor to share the workload and the risk. Equally important, a knowledgeable partner can help determine the property's existing and after-repair value more accurately than a beginning investor. Plus, an experienced contractor can help prevent the underestimation of improvement costs and keep new flippers from getting in over their heads. Veteran investors should know what to fix, based on the expected return, and the features that other houses for sale offer. They should also have the resources to get the work done quickly at a fair price.

When forming a partnership, always clarify roles and expectations in writing. Include a project budget, how many hours are expected from the partners, and if partners' hours will be billed as an additional cost to the project. Lastly, check your partner's credentials and referrals. If possible, inspect previous projects.

Retailers are limited by their financial resources and the number of properties they can rehab at once. Each deal should be evaluated separately; it can be sound business to act as a dealer at some times and as a retailer at other times.

FIND THE BACK DOOR FIRST

Every investor should have a means to sell properties quickly. Don't enter into a real estate transaction without knowing your exit strategy. Are you going to flip the property to another investor, or are you going to fix it up and sell it retail? How much money or labor will you put into the property? How long do you expect to hold it? How long do you think it will take to sell? Answer these questions *before* you make an offer to purchase a property.

When you are getting started, you can sell your first few deals to investors to generate working capital. You should not be greedy, but you can expect to make $1,000 to $3,000 on your first flip. You do not have to own a property to make money from it; you simply need to control it by putting it under contract. Once you have located a potential deal and secured it with a purchase contract, you can sell your deal to another investor for a profit.

Example: Selling to Another Investor

You find a property worth about $100,000 in its current state. Renovations will require $10,000. In its best condition, the property is worth $115,000. You negotiate a purchase price of $80,000 and sign a purchase contract with the owner. You find another investor who is willing to pay $82,000 for the property and do the necessary repairs. Thus, you can sell your deal to another investor and walk away with a $2,000 profit using no money of your own. The other investor will make a nice profit as well.

In this example, the property was purchased at a 20 percent discount from its current market value. This discount may vary widely, depending on the property, the neighborhood, the condition of your local real estate market, and how many repairs the property needs. (We will discuss a precise approach to making offers later in Chapter 6.)

Keep in mind that the retailer to whom you sell the property will make more money than you on the deal. Don't let that person's profit potential bother you. There is enough room for both of you to profit, and, unlike a retailer, you assume little risk.

JOIN AN INVESTMENT CLUB

A real estate investors club in your area is an excellent place to meet other dealers and retailers. A complete list of local groups can be found at http://www.creonline.com/clubs.htm. If no clubs are in your area, consider forming one. You can find other local investors by reading the classified ads section of your newspaper under the "Real Estate Wanted" and "Private Money to Loan" sections. You can also run a classified ad under the "Investment Properties" section. In addition, ask some local real estate agents and landlords or apartment associations for names of investors in your community.

RUN A CLASSIFIED AD

If you have a property under contract and are looking for a retailer, run a classified ad in a local newspaper. Try a few different newspapers and ads. (See Appendix B for sample ads.) Use the Internet to expand your advertising base. Some Web sites will advertise your property for little or no cost. Log the calls you receive to track the effectiveness of the ad. More important, keep information about the people who call and the types of properties they like. Don't waste too much time with inexperienced investors, because they probably don't have the means to buy properties from you.

Qualify the callers by asking the following questions:

- How many houses do you buy each year?
- What type of discount do you usually look for on properties?
- Do you have your own cash to close or will you borrow it?
- How big a renovation can you handle?
- If I find a bargain, how quickly can you close?

Asking these questions will quickly generate a list of investors to call when a new project comes along. If you don't have an investment club in your area, use this method to meet other investors.

SELLING PROPERTIES RETAIL

Many beginning investors try to sell a property without a real estate agent to save money on commissions. They also neglect to include the agent's commission in their estimate of costs for the property. If you are selling a property retail to an owner-occupant, failing to use an agent is a mistake. In fact, a majority of sellers who start out selling their properties without agents end up listing the properties with agents after being unsuccessful on their own.

Most real estate agents don't aggressively market properties; however, they place the information on the multiple listing service (MLS) used by all other real estate agents. Because most properties are sold through the MLS and the largest pool of qualified buyers work through real estate agents, the odds of finding a qualified buyer quickly are greatest when the property is listed on the MLS. That approach allows you to focus your efforts on finding more deals rather than waiting for buyers to show up at your property.

Contrary to what agents would like you to believe, most do little to market your particular property other than post a colorful sign and list the property on the MLS. Today, you have several options to list your property on the MLS without paying full brokerage fees. Many areas have programs that let the seller take on some of the responsibilities that were once handled exclusively by real estate agents in exchange for a lower fee. Internet Web sites such as http://www.forsalebyowner.com have created additional options for listing properties for a lower price. However, if you are inexperienced, you may consider hiring a full-service real estate agent on your first few deals. As your advocate when negotiating offers, your agent will make sure the contracts are in order and executed according to plan. Indeed, an agent's actions can make or break a deal. Find one you like to work with who is willing to give you a discount for repeat business and help you find other potential deals. If you are doing business in a state in which the real estate agents draft the purchase contract, make sure your agent is competent and experienced and can guide you through the paperwork as a beginning investor. In some cases, it may be cheaper and more effective to use a low-cost listing service and hire an attorney to help you through the details.

Not every property can be resold or flipped quickly. You may get stuck with a property for a few months, but this rarely happens if you do your homework. If you cannot resell a property within 30 days, you probably made a mistake—you either paid too much, underestimated repairs, or picked the wrong neighborhood.

GETTING RID OF DIFFICULT PROPERTIES

Sometimes you may sign up a marginal deal and have a difficult time reselling it. Even though you want quick cash, you can find other ways to make a profit. For example, you can take a promissory note (a written, legal promise to pay) from your investor-buyer for part or the entire purchase price. You would secure this note with a lien on the property with interest payments. (The lien would be a mortgage or deed of trust, as we will discuss in Chapter 2.) Or you can tell the investor you will accept a promissory note for the purchase price with no payments due until the investor resells the property. If a deal is thin and needs a lot of work, the retailer who buys it may not have enough cash to pay you. In that case, become partners with that retailer. If you are flipping to an investor who will rehab the property, you can offer the property as your share of the partnership, while the investor offers the materials and the work as his or her share. When you sell the property, you split the proceeds. It's possible you may have to take less than half of the net profit to make the deal work. (In the chapters ahead, you'll learn lots of creative ways to move properties.)

MINIMIZE YOUR LOSS

Sometimes you sign a purchase contract for a "bad" house that you cannot sell for a reasonable profit. The problem may be a combination of paying too much, bad market timing, unforeseen repairs, or just plain bad luck. Keep in mind that you can always sell the house for what you paid or even take a loss if you have a lot of cash invested. Sometimes you have to move on and stop the financial bleeding.

Remember that when you make an offer, you have to include enough room in the deal for someone other than you to make a profit. (See Chapter 4.) Many beginners make this mistake. You cannot resell a property to another investor and make a profit if the investor cannot profit as well. If you want too much profit and hold on to a property too long, you can lose out in the long run. When you are flipping properties as a dealer, the goal is to move them fast—don't get greedy! You will learn how to make money in all types of markets. Do your homework and go into every deal prepared. Then you will come out ahead.

KEY POINTS TO REMEMBER

- A flipper buys property with the intent of quick resale.

- There are three types of flippers: the scout, the dealer, and the retailer.

- A flipper may act as a dealer on some transactions and a retailer on others.

- Establish a network of other investors to buy your properties.

- Use the MLS to sell your retail properties.

- Learn how to make money in a changing market.

- Cut your losses on bad deals.

2

THE MECHANICS OF REAL ESTATE TRANSACTIONS

Whether you are a novice investor or an experienced one, you must have a working knowledge of the legal aspects of real estate transactions. It's critical to understand the paperwork involved in a real estate transaction. Otherwise, you are at the mercy of those who do know. Furthermore, your risk of making an expensive mistake or missing an opportunity increases tremendously.

THE DEED

A deed is a written instrument used to convey ownership to property. You must know how to draft a deed, because at times you may need to get one signed in a hurry. If you are dealing with a seller in foreclosure, a "kitchen table" deed is commonly used, so you need to know how to draft and execute one. If another investor is offering you a deed received from someone in foreclosure across a kitchen table, you must make sure that deed was drafted and executed properly.

Does Your State Require a Cooling Off Period?

Some states have prohibitions on getting a deed from a seller in foreclosure without certain disclosures and a cooling off period. At the time of this printing, those states include California, Maryland, Minnesota, and Missouri, but other states are considering similar legislation. Check your state law to make sure you are in compliance.

TYPES OF DEEDS

Deeds differ, usually by the type of guarantee or warranty that they give. Following are descriptions of four different types of deeds: general warranty, special warranty, bargain and sale, and quitclaim.

General Warranty Deed

Also referred to as a warranty deed, this is the most complete guarantee of title. The warranty deed promises that the grantor (seller) has full and complete title and forever warrants against any claims against the title. If anyone makes a claim to the property, no matter how old the claim is, the grantor of a warranty deed must fix the problem. If you are receiving a deed, you must insist on getting a general warranty deed. There are exceptions to this rule, but a general warranty deed is the best deed. If a title company is insuring the transaction, it will probably insist on having a warranty deed.

Special Warranty Deed

This type of deed only warrants that the grantor has acquired title and did nothing to impair it while holding the title. This is roughly the equivalent of a grant deed (used in California). Public officials, such as a sheriff, use a special warranty deed after a foreclosure sale.

Bargain and Sale Deed

This type of deed has no express warranties but usually contains a statement of consideration paid and an implication that the grantor has some title or interest in the property. This deed is commonly used with variation in northeastern states such as New York and New Jersey.

Quitclaim Deed

A quitclaim deed contains no promises or warranties. The grantor simply gives up whatever claim he or she may or may not have. A quitclaim deed is commonly used to transfer an interest between spouses or to clear up a title defect. A seller with a good title can transfer the property with a quitclaim deed the same as with a warranty deed. However, the grantor makes no guarantee that title is good. You should consider using a quitclaim deed whenever you give title.

ELEMENTS OF THE DEED

A deed must contain certain elements to be considered a legal and valid transfer. When you execute a deed or pay someone else for a deed to real estate, make sure that the following elements are present.

In Writing

Generally speaking, any instrument affecting an interest in real estate must be in writing to be enforceable. It does not necessarily need to be typed, but it may not be accepted for public recording if it is not legible.

Parties to the Transaction

The deed must state the giver of the deed (grantor) and the receiver of the deed (grantee). The grantor's name must be spelled exactly as it appears on the deed that gave that person title, even if that spelling is incorrect. In community property states (Arizona, California, Florida, Idaho, Louisiana, Nevada, New Mexico, Texas, and Washington), the law presumes that both spouses own all marital assets, regardless of how they are titled. Thus, you also need a separate quitclaim deed from the grantor's spouse, even if that person's name does not appear on the title.

Consideration

The deed must state that the grantor received consideration, even if no actual money changed hands. You can insert the purchase price or simply the words: "The grantee has received ten dollars in hand and other good and valuable consideration, the sufficiency of which is hereby acknowledged."

Legal Description

The legal description of the property must appear exactly as in the previous deed. It will usually read something like "Lot 25, Block 21, Harris Subdivision, County of Barrington, State of Illinois." This designation comes from a plat map that was previously filed in the county records. If the description is more complicated than a simple lot and block or government survey description, simply photocopy the description from the previous deed and insert it into the new deal.

Words of Conveyance

This language spells out what type of deed is given. It usually reads something like, "The grantor hereby grants, conveys, and warrants" (warranty deed) or "the grantor hereby remises, releases, and quitclaims" (quitclaim deed).

Signature of the Grantor

The grantor must sign his or her name exactly as it appears above in the document. If the grantor is not available for signature, an authorized agent or attorney-in-fact may sign on the grantor's behalf. This process is accomplished by a power of attorney that authorizes an agent to act for the grantor to sign a deed. The power of attorney should include a legal description of the property and should be recorded in county records with the deed that is signed by the agent. The agent does not sign the grantor's name but rather signs his or her own name as attorney-in-fact for the grantor.

Acknowledgment

The deed should be acknowledged before a notary public. An acknowledgment is a declaration that the person signing is who he or she claims to be and is signing voluntarily. The notary signs the deed, affirming that the grantor appeared and that the notary either knows the person or was provided with sufficient proof of identity. Although acknowledgment is not required to make a deed valid, it is usually required for recording. The proper form of acknowledgment differs from state to state, so make certain your deed complies with your state's law.

Have a Notary on Call

Often, you will buy a property with a seller signing a deed over a kitchen table. Because the signature of the seller must be notarized, you need to have a notary on call. Look in your local phone book under "Notary Publics." Virtually every city has a notary with a pager who will show up on 30 minutes' notice.

DELIVERY

Title does not pass until a deed is delivered to the grantee. Thus, a deed signed but held in escrow does not convey title until the escrow agent delivers the deed. Many people are under the mistaken impression that title passes when a deed is recorded. While recording a deed is common practice, it is not required to convey title to real estate.

RECORDING DOCUMENTS

The recording system gives constructive notice to the public of the transfer of an interest in property. Recording simply involves bringing the original document to the local county courthouse or county clerk's office. The original document is copied onto a computer or microfiche and then returned to the new owner. In addition, the county tax assessor usually requires filing a "real property transfer declaration," which contains basic information about the sale. The filing fee for recording the deed usually runs $6 to $10 per page. In addition, the county, city, and/or state may assess a transfer tax based on either the value of the property or the selling price (often called documentary stamps).

A deed or other conveyance does not have to be recorded to be a valid transfer of an interest. For example, if John gives a deed to Mary, then he gives it again to Fred, who records it first? Or if John gives a mortgage to ABC Savings & Loan but the mortgage is not filed for six months, and then John borrows from another lender, who records the mortgage first? Who wins and who loses in these scenarios?

Most states follow a race-notice rule, which means that the first person to record the document wins, as long as he or she

- received title in good faith,
- paid value, and
- had no notice of a prior transfer.

Example: Who Holds the First Mortgage?

John buys a home by borrowing $75,000 from ABC Savings & Loan. He signs a promissory note and a mortgage pledging his home as collateral. ABC messes up the paperwork, and the mortgage does not get recorded for 18 months. In the interim, John borrows $12,000 from XYZ Mortgage Company, for which he gives a mortgage as collateral. XYZ Mortgage Company records its mortgage, unaware of John's unrecorded first mortgage to ABC Savings & Loan. As a result, XYZ Mortgage Company will have a first mortgage on the property.

NOTES AND MORTGAGES

Most people think of going to a bank to get a mortgage. Actually, people go to the bank to get a loan. Once they are approved for the loan, they sign a promissory note to the lender, which is their promise to pay. They also give (not get) a mortgage as security for repayment of the note. A mortgage (also called a deed of trust in some states) is a security agreement under which the borrower pledges the property as collateral for payment. The mortgage document is recorded in the property records, creating a lien on the property in favor of the lender.

If the underlying obligation (the promissory note) is paid off, the lender must release the collateral (the mortgage). A release is accomplished by signing a release of mortgage, which is recorded in the county property records. The release will remove the mortgage lien from the property. If you search the public records of a particular property, you will see many recorded mortgages that have been placed and released over the years.

Deed of Trust

About half the states use a document called a deed of trust rather than a mortgage. The deed of trust is a document in which the trustor (borrower) gives a deed to a neutral third party (trustee) to hold for the beneficiary (lender). A deed of trust is worded almost the same as a mortgage. Thus, the deed of trust and the mortgage are essentially the same, other than in the foreclosure process. Foreclosure is a legal proceeding by which a lender attempts to force the sale of a property to recoup the money lent to the homeowner.

PRIORITY OF LIENS

Liens, like deeds, are "first in time, first in line." If a property is owned free and clear, a mortgage recorded will be a first mortgage. A mortgage recorded later in time will be a second mortgage (sometimes called a junior mortgage). Likewise, any judgments or other liens recorded later are also junior liens. Holding a first mortgage is a desirable position, because a foreclosure on a mortgage can wipe out all liens that are recorded after it (called junior lien holders). (We will discuss foreclosures in detail in Chapter 3.)

THE BASIC LOAN TRANSACTION

At the closing of a typical real estate sale, the seller conveys a deed to the buyer. Buyers usually obtain loans from conventional lenders for most of the cash needed for the purchase price. As discussed earlier, the lender gives the buyer cash to pay the seller, and the buyer gives the lender a promissory note. The buyer also gives the lender a security instrument (mortgage or deed of trust) under which the buyer pledges the property as collateral. When the transaction is complete, the buyer has the title recorded in their name, and the lender has a lien recorded against the property.

TYPICAL OWNER-CARRY TRANSACTION

Rather than receiving all cash for the purchase price, a seller may accept a promissory note for all or part of the price. If the seller owns the property free and clear (i.e., no mortgage) and accepts a promissory note for all or part of the purchase price, the buyer will execute a mortgage or deed of trust to the seller. When the transaction is complete, the buyer has the title recorded in the buyer's name and the seller has a lien (mortgage or deed of trust) on the property.

In some cases, the seller may already have a mortgage on the property. If this is the case, the seller may require the buyer to pay most of the purchase price in the form of cash so that the seller can satisfy the loan balance. The difference between the loan balance and the purchase price (equity) is paid in the form

FIGURE 2.1 *Typical Owner Carry*

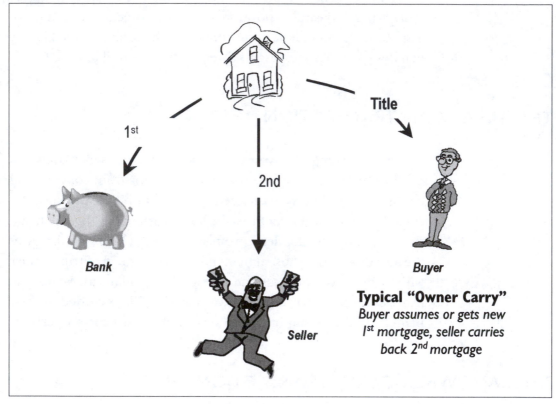

of a promissory note. Assuming the buyer borrows the cash from a conventional lender, the note to the seller will be secured by a mortgage that is junior or subordinate to the lender's mortgage. When the transaction is complete and all documents are recorded, the buyer has title recorded in the buyer's name, the lender has a first lien, and the seller has a second lien on the property, as shown in Figure 2.1.

ASSUMABLE VERSUS NONASSUMABLE MORTGAGES

Some properties have freely assumable mortgages; that is, the buyer does not have to qualify with a lender to take over the seller's loan. Buying a property with an assumable mortgage is desirable for two reasons. First, the buyer does not need good credit to qualify for the loan. Second, the buyer does not have to pay the costs (several thousand dollars) associated with obtaining a new loan. Because the buyer is an investor, it almost seems a crime for the buyer to pay these loan costs when he or she will resell the property within a few months and pay off the balance of the loan.

THE DUE-ON-SALE CLAUSE

Many years ago, all loans were freely assumable, meaning anyone could purchase property by taking title and making payments on the existing loan. When interest rates began rising, lenders were competing with existing low-interest loans. Some banker figured out that this competition could be eliminated by placing restrictions on the transfer of property encumbered by a mortgage. Thus the due-on-sale clause was created.

The due-on-sale clause contained in a mortgage or deed of trust gives the lender the option to require complete payoff (acceleration) of the underlying loan if the property is sold or if the title is transferred. Most loans insured by the Federal Housing Authority (FHA) that originated before December 15, 1989, and loans guaranteed by the Department of Veterans Affairs (VA) that originated before March 1, 1988, are freely assumable; that is, these mortgages have no due-on-sale clauses. However, virtually all loans today contain due-on-sale clauses. If you take title to a property without paying off the loan, the bank has the right to call the loan due.

Contrary to urban myth, it is not a criminal act to transfer property with a mortgage containing a due-on-sale clause. A mortgage is simply a contract between the lender and the borrower, the breach of which gives the lender the right to call the loan due. The loan acceleration is not automatic; the lender has the option of doing so or not. If the lender does call the loan due and it is not paid off, the lender has the option of foreclosing the property.

Banks rarely enforce the due-on-sale clause anymore because the process of calling in loans that are performing is not profitable. When interest rates were high, it made financial sense for a bank to call in a 6 percent loan, forcing the borrower to refinance. However, the market interest rates are still relatively low, so it would not be profitable for a lender to call a loan due, especially if the payments are current. If market interest rates remain equal to or less than the rate of the loan you are concerned about being called due, chances are you will have no objection from the lender.

Many people who own real property subject to a trust deed simply transfer it, figuring the lender (which, after all, may be a large corporation on the other side of the country) won't find out. They are often right.

Third-party servicing companies handle the payments on most loans today. Thus, there is little chance that anyone pays close attention to the name on the checks received for the monthly payments. Even if you get caught, chances are you will sell the property before the lender can call the loan due.

THE DOUBLE CLOSING

As we will discuss in Chapter 8, a closing is a ceremonial process during which title is delivered by deed from the seller to the buyer. In some cases, you will buy and sell the property to a retailer in a back-to-back double closing (also called double escrow in some states). You do not need any of your own cash to purchase the property from the owner before reselling it to the retailer in a double closing.

Here's how it works in eight steps:

1. The dealer signs a written agreement to purchase a property from the owner.
2. The dealer signs a written contract with the retailer under which the retailer agrees to buy the property from the dealer at a higher price.
3. The only party coming to the table with cash is the retailer. Assuming the retailer is borrowing money from a lender to fund the transaction, the retailer's bank will wire the funds into the bank account of the attorney, escrow agent, or title company (called the closing agent) who performs the closing.
4. The owner signs a deed to the dealer, which is not delivered but deposited in escrow with the closing agent.
5. The dealer signs a deed to the retailer that is deposited in escrow with the closing agent.
6. The retailer signs the bank loan documents, at which point the transaction is complete.
7. The closing agent delivers the funds to the owner for the purchase price and delivers the difference to the dealer.
8. The closing agent records the two deeds, one after another, at the county land records office.

As you can see, the dealer brought no cash to the table and received funds from the proceeds of the second sale. If the second sale does not happen, the first transaction, which is closed in escrow, is not complete. The deal is dead.

The so-called "illegal property-flipping schemes" work like this. Unscrupulous investors buy cheap, run-down properties in mostly low-income neighborhoods. They do shoddy renovations to the properties and sell them to unsophisticated buyers at inflated prices. In most cases, the investor, appraiser, and mortgage broker conspire by submitting fraudulent loan documents and a

> ### Flipping Is Not Illegal
>
> Since writing this book in 2001, we've received hundreds of e-mails from people asking, "Isn't flipping illegal?" In the past few years, there has been a lot of negative press and misinformation about double closings. Many people have been indicted under what the press has labeled "property-flipping scams." Misinformed lenders, real estate agents, and title companies will tell you that double closings are now illegal. In fact, they are not.

bogus appraisal. The result? The buyer pays too much for a house and cannot afford the loan. Because many of these loans are insured by the Federal Housing Authority (FHA), the government authorities have investigated this practice and arrested many of the parties involved.

Despite the negative press, neither flipping nor double closings are illegal. The activities described above amount to loan fraud, nothing more. The media has inappropriately reported the activity as illegal "property flipping" rather than "loan fraud." So whenever you hear a real estate agent or mortgage broker say that flipping is illegal, you know they are misinformed.

Unfortunately, this misunderstanding has not been without consequences. Many title and escrow companies will not do double closings anymore because of the risk of *potential* fraud. Other title companies simply require all parties to sign additional disclosures, so that all parties understand the transaction involves two closings, the second of which will fund the first.

TITLE SEASONING

Some lenders have placed seasoning requirements on the seller's ownership. That means if the seller has not owned the property for at least six months, the lender will assume that the deal is fishy and refuse to fund the buyer's loan. This may be a problem if you bought a property at a low price and are reselling it quickly for a profit, and even more of a problem if you are double closing. However, lender guidelines are not law; they are just guidelines. By going up the chain of command, you can generally get approval from loan underwriting. It's up to you to prove that the property is being resold for a higher price because either it was purchased in a distress situation (e.g., foreclosure) or substantial repairs were made. Keep good records of your repairs to show to the lender.

A smart investor stays on top of the process and anticipates these issues. If you are buying a property and reselling it quickly, particularly in a double closing situation, be sure to anticipate this problem and deal with it. Let the buyer and his or her real estate agent and lender know there may be a seasoning issue. If you stay in control of the loan process and steer your buyers to a mortgage company that doesn't have a problem with double closings, then seasoning won't become an issue. Generally speaking, only FHA and subprime lenders have the "seasoning hang-up." Fannie Mae underwriting guidelines don't prohibit funding a purchase money loan when the seller has not owned the property for a minimum period of time.

FHA ANTIFLIPPING REGULATIONS

Part of the "flipping is illegal" hoopla is a result of the Federal Housing Authority's new antiflipping regulations. FHA regulations, which are part of federal law, prohibit the funding of a purchase in which the seller has not owned the property for at least 90 days—no exceptions. Also, if the seller has owned the property between 91 and 180 days, and the new sales price exceeds the previous sales price by 100 percent or more, the lender will require additional documentation validating the property's value.

If the buyer is getting an FHA-insured loan, there is no way around the seasoning issue. This generally should not be a problem in a fix-and-flip situation, because your ownership will likely extend past 90 days by the time you acquire, rehab, and sell. But if you are planning to buy the property and resell it in a double closing, the end buyer cannot go with an FHA loan. If your end buyer is another investor, he or she will not be using FHA financing, so this should not present a problem. (Note: Don't confuse FHA-insured loans with FNMA, or Fannie Mae, loans. FHA loans represent a small portion of residential loans, as compared with Fannie Mae loans, which are the majority of residential loans. Fannie Mae does not have seasoning restrictions.)

DEED RESTRICTIONS

Once in a while, a seller may place a deed restriction that prevents the buyer from reselling within a certain time period. This restriction is a covenant in the deed, which cannot be circumvented because no title company will insure it. You may find this in new subdivisions, particularly in condominium complexes where the developer is trying to prohibit flippers.

ASSIGNMENT OF CONTRACT

Another way to accomplish the same task as a double closing is to assign your purchase contract. Assigning a contract is similar to double-endorsing a check—you assign your rights under the contract to another investor for a fee. The investor closes directly with the owner in your place, like a pinch hitter. This is also a solution to the lender seasoning issue. If the buyer closes directly with the owner, the seasoning issue is resolved.

Contracts with a Prohibition against Assignment

An assignment will not work if the seller has a standard contract that contains a prohibition against assignment, commonly found with bank-owned or government-owned properties. In such cases, you can still do a double closing with one small catch—if the seller selects the title or escrow company (this is common with bank- and government-owned properties), that title or escrow company may not permit double closings. No solution to this problem exists, but you should be aware of it up front so you can avoid problems later.

Advantages of Using Assignments

Using the contract assignment has several advantages over a double closing. First, your name does not appear on the title for the world to see, allowing your business affairs to be kept private, as they should be. Furthermore, the sale at a lower price does not appear on the MLS, which can skew the appraisal when the retailer resells the property. (See the discussion on appraisals in Chapter 4.) Also, you save on closing costs by not having a regular closing. Finally, you get your money fast, whether or not the other investor closes on the property. (Note: The assignment will not prevent the FHA flipping ban, because FHA rules say the seller must be the "owner of record.")

Disadvantages of Using Assignments

The main disadvantage of the contract assignment is that it is hard to sell. A closing is usually conducted at a title company or attorney's office, while a contract assignment may not be. Unless the investor knows you personally, he or she may be wary of buying your contract. The contract assignment requires the investor to conduct due diligence regarding the title to the property, the legality of the contract, and whether the seller will live up to it at closing time. Thus, you may not get as much money for a contract assignment as you would if you did a double closing and gave the investor a bona fide deed.

The second disadvantage of the contract assignment is that the investor knows what you are paying for the property. An unscrupulous investor may try to go around you and deal directly with the property owner. The solution to this challenge is to record a Memorandum of Agreement in county land records. (See the sample form in Appendix C.) This form is an affidavit signed by you that states you have a contract with the seller. Once recorded, this affidavit becomes a cloud on the seller's title. A cloud is an uncertainty regarding ownership. This uncertainty makes it difficult to insure the title. (As discussed in Chapter 8, getting title insurance may be a necessary part of a real estate transaction.)

If the seller and the unscrupulous investor try to close the deal, the title company would discover the cloud on the seller's title and would probably refuse to insure the transaction. The cloud on title will effectively prevent the seller from selling the property to anyone but you, the party the seller originally agreed to sell the property to. In this situation, the seller or the unscrupulous investor would have to pay you ransom to step out of the deal (which, by the way, is done by you signing a quitclaim deed).

KEY POINTS TO REMEMBER

- Understand the basic mechanics of real estate transactions

- Use double closings and contract assignments to flip properties

- Be aware of potential seasoning and flipping issues

3

PROVEN WAYS TO FIND THE DEALS

In Chapter 1, we discussed the importance of buying distressed properties, which in reality means finding distressed owners. Locating these owners is an art that takes years to master. Finding motivated sellers requires advertising, marketing, salesmanship, and, like any business, keeping your nose to the ground. Over time, wise investors establish a referral network, which allows them to find more deals with less effort.

The most common problem new investors face is finding bargain properties. Many who start out in real estate investing quit without ever buying their first property. They go through the motions of looking for deals for a few weeks or months, then decide it doesn't work. They forget that finding motivated sellers is similar to a salesperson's finding that first customer—it takes persistence and hard work.

You cannot put together a deal without a motivated seller, and you can convince only a motivated seller to accept unusual terms or sell at a discounted price. A motivated seller has a pressing reason to sell the property below market price. Before you start looking for motivated sellers, first realize that the vast majority of property owners are not motivated to sell.

FIND MOTIVATED SELLERS

At the risk of sounding redundant, the concept is simple: find motivated sellers who are willing to sell their properties at a discounted price. Currently, the real estate market in most parts of the country is healthy, though it appears to be slowing somewhat. Many people are complaining that the strength of the market precludes investors from finding deals on properties. The popular misconception is that in a rising market, even the most motivated sellers can find buyers for their property at full market price.

The truth is, you can work the concept of flipping properties in any market. (We will address finding profitable deals in changing markets in detail in Chapter 11.) Real estate legend A.D. Kessler once said, "There are no problem properties, just problem ownerships." The definition of a motivated seller fits squarely within Kessler's idea. A logical person knows that time, money, and effort can solve virtually any real estate problem. However, some people are too emotional about their real estate problems or have other motivating issues to deal with.

Some of the issues that motivate people to sell include:

- Divorce
- Lack of concern
- Inexperience with real estate repairs
- Time constraints
- Death of a loved one
- Job transfer
- The headaches of being a landlord
- Impending foreclosure and other financial problems

In conclusion, if you deal only with motivated sellers, you will be able to negotiate the right price and terms.

USE THE NEWSPAPER

An obvious, yet often overlooked, place to look for deals is in your local newspaper in the "Real Estate Classified" section. Internet-based classified ads are one category in this strategy. Just follow the same approach when identifying and approaching motivated sellers from either source. Be prepared to make a lot of calls, because finding properties is a numbers game. Do not waste much time with each seller; just ask basic questions to gather information about the property and the seller's needs. (We will discuss the right questions to ask in Chapter 5.) Most people you call cold out of the paper will not be responsive. Don't take it personally; just keep calling. Remember that each time you hear a no, you will be one call closer to a yes, and you will be learning along the way. If you live in a large metropolitan area, start with the ads for the areas you know. If you live in a more rural area, call every ad in the newspaper.

Private Owner Ads

Call on the ads that are for sale by owner. (They don't all say "for sale by owner," but you will learn to detect these by other clues.) You will notice that real estate agents place many of the ads. Most areas require that real estate agents identify their licensed status within the ad. However, agents often ignore that requirement. You do not need to call on most of those ads, for there is a better way to deal with real estate agents (as we will discuss in the following section).

If you are not inspired to call on every ad, then at a minimum, call on the ads with key phrases. Examples of these key phrases are *must sell, fix-up, needs work, handyman special, vacant, motivated,* and so on. Unusually long ads listing every detail about the property are probably from inexperienced or motivated sellers, so these ads also warrant a call.

Real Estate Agent Ads

Believe it or not, many of the ads placed by real estate agents are teaser ads designed to get you calling about a particular type of house or neighborhood in which the agent works. Agents often pull the old bait-and-switch. Once you call, they try to get you into their office so they can show you other properties.

If the ad is for a property in one of your target neighborhoods, then call the agent for a different reason—to let this agent know what kinds of properties you like. Call on all of the ads that advertise fixer properties in your target areas and ask for the agents' e-mail addresses and fax numbers. Send these agents a brief letter, alerting them that you are an investor, you are looking for fixer properties, and you can close quickly if the price is right. (You'll find a sample fax, which you can format as an e-mail, in Appendix B.) Send this letter to no fewer than 25 real estate offices in your first month of doing business. This letter will get the agents calling you for properties, rather than the other way around.

Properties for Rent

Another way to find deals is by calling the classified ads offering houses for rent. Most cities have more properties for rent than for sale. One reason is that some people become accidental landlords for one reason or another. For example, they may have inherited the property from their parents, or the owner may be recently widowed and their spouse had handled the properties. These people rent out the properties because they don't know what else to do with them.

Calling rental ads can be lucrative, because some landlords are simply tired of dealing with tenant and property management issues. These landlords may want a way out of handling their problem property. You just don't know what the landlord's needs are until you ask, so consider calling on these ads for rent. Just pick up the phone and say, "I saw your ad in the paper for a property you are renting. I am an investor. Are you interested in selling the property?" When the answer is no, give these landlords your name and telephone number and ask them to call you when they decide to sell. Also, ask them if they know any other landlords in the area who may be interested in selling.

Making a lot of telephone calls does not excite most people, but the telephone can make you a lot of money. (We will discuss telephone negotiating further in Chapter 5.)

Run Your Own Classified Ad

Run your own newspaper ad in the "Real Estate Classified" section to encourage motivated owners to call you. Many distressed sellers won't take the time or make the effort to advertise their property, so you need to flush them out. Run a simple three-line ad, such as:

We Buy Houses for Cash
Any Condition, Fast Closing
555-555-5555

Run this ad under the "Real Estate Wanted" section in the major newspapers and small, local all-advertisement papers, such as

Pennysaver and *Thrifty Nickel.* You can also run it under "Money to Loan" to attract property owners in foreclosure. (You will find other sample ads in Appendix B.)

Classified ads should be run every day of the week, not just on Sundays. Call your newspaper and ask for the bulk or long-term rate. This rate may require you to commit to six months or more of advertising. You should consider running the ad for at least six months to determine whether it is worthwhile. Do not be discouraged if you see seven other ads just like yours. McDonald's and Burger King do more business when they are next door to each other; so do home-improvement giants such as Home Depot and Lowe's. Likewise, your ad will pull just as many calls next to similar ads. Sometimes a motivated seller will choose to do business with you over someone else because of the sound of your voice or the fact that you like the Yankees. You just never know what motivates people, so place your ad in the newspaper and keep it there.

The 800-Pound Gorilla

You may have seen bright yellow billboards that say "We Buy Ugly Houses." The company, HomeVestors of America, Inc. based in Dallas, Texas, is a franchise operation that spends a lot of money advertising on radio, billboards, and even television. The numbers vary from city to city, but we've been told that some franchisees collectively spend as much as $100,000 per month on advertising in some cities. That's a very large budget to compete with, but don't worry—some consumers like dealing with the "big guys" and some will do business with you because you are a "little guy." In some sense, large operations like this are competition, but in another sense, they create market awareness for a service that helps you do more business as well.

Call Other Ads Yourself

As discussed in Chapter 1, dealers need to find a pool of retail investors to whom they can sell their properties. The "We Buy Houses" ads are a great place to find these people.

Unless you have a business office, set up a separate telephone line in your home to handle incoming calls. If you are not available during the day to answer calls, have the calls forwarded to your cell phone. (Don't even consider *not* having a cell phone.) If you are working full-time at another profession, use a voice mail that screens out potentially motivated sellers. For example, the messages could say: "Thank you for calling Real Estate Solutions, Inc. If you are calling about a house for sale, please leave your name, telephone number, the property address, and why you are selling." This message screens out the truly motivated sellers from the marginally motivated sellers who are simply looking to shop their properties.

When calling others, or receiving calls, it makes sense to develop a script to use—especially when you are new to the flipping business. Be honest with sellers and let them know you are not a large company. You can explain that you take a personal interest in their specific needs and circumstances. Also mention that you have the resources to handle cash transactions, while your low overhead allows you to pay a fair price for their property. It is okay to gather information about the property and establish that the seller is motivated. However, it is best to minimize the discussion. Use the call to set up a personal meeting.

REAL ESTATE AGENTS

Real estate agents can be either a great source of potential deals or a big stumbling block, depending on how you deal with them. They are among the most informed people regarding properties for sale, and they have access to more information than investors do. Agents also have many contacts and may know of potential deals that are not advertised on the MLS (called pocket listings).

Much of the information that was once exclusively available to MLS subscribers is now available to anyone with Internet access. However, consumer real estate sites are not typically as good as the sites real estate agents can access. The agents-only sites provide better search engines and more data; they are also usually updated more frequently than consumer sites. Although the gap has narrowed, real estate agents still have the upper hand in watching market activity.

Agent versus Broker

In most states, a person must be licensed as a broker to list property. A listing is an agreement between the seller and the broker that permits the broker to sell the property for a fee. In most cases, this fee is 6 or 7 percent of the sales price. The broker who signs this agreement with the seller is called the listing broker or sometimes the managing broker.

The listing broker usually hires several agents (sometimes called salespersons) to help sell their listed properties. An agent, like a broker, must be licensed to sell real estate. In most states, however, only a broker can list a property. Thus, if the agent finds a buyer for the property, the listing broker and the agent split the commission for the sale. While a broker and an agent are different, this book refers to them synonymously as *agent.* (Note: Each state has its own requirements for agent commissions, so learn about your state's requirements.)

Agents can also represent buyers or sellers in different capacities, such as buyer's agent/broker, seller's agent/broker, or transaction agent/broker. Some states actually require attorneys to provide services that are offered by agents in most of the country. It pays to understand the various agency relationships allowed in your area.

What Is a Realtor?

REALTOR® is a registered trademark term reserved only for members of the local board of Realtors, which is affiliated with the National Association of Realtors. The boards are private, self-regulating agencies that govern rules of conduct for their members. Most agents belong to one or more local boards; membership is usually a requirement to obtain access to the MLS computer system.

Real estate agents can earn additional designations. Typically, serious agents will undergo continuing education to earn such titles as Graduate Realtor Institute (GRI), Council of Residential Specialists (CRS), or a multitude of others. When evaluating potential agents, ask about their credentials and why they chose a specific educational track. Of course, formal education is only one way to assess your agent's value and does not guarantee that the individual has the skills you need.

The Buyer's Agent

A buyer's agent represents a buyer looking for properties. Most listing agents will offer a co-op fee to any buyer's agent who procures a buyer to purchase the property. This co-op is a part of the listing agent's commission.

The buyers' agent's loyalty and representation belong to the buyer, although the buyer's agent is paid by the listing agent. Because buyers' agents usually procure the buyers to make the sale, they are often referred to as the selling agents.

Example: Agents' Commissions

A property is listed at $100,000 on the MLS. The listing agent's commission is 7 percent and he is offering a 3 percent co-op fee. The listing agent's fee would be $7,000 if he found a buyer for the property. If a buyer's agent found the buyer, and the property was sold for $100,000, then the listing agent would get $4,000, and the buyer's agent would get $3,000.

Using a good buyer's agent will help you find a lot of deals. The agent can check the MLS for new properties for sale on a regular basis. Also, ask your agent to search through the MLS for the motivation buzzwords, such as *must sell, needs work, estate sale, fore-closure, divorce, rehab,* and so on. These buzzwords will locate distressed properties. Remember, distressed properties are those that create emotional or financial distress for their owners.

Make offers only on the distressed properties that are already priced below market. You may find it hard to believe, but many agents list properties in need of work at full market price. In addition, ask your agent to search the MLS in your target areas by price per square foot, which can also generate leads for bargains.

Although a buyer's agent can be an excellent source of leads, don't use the agent as your primary source of leads when you get started. Agents are businesspeople and their time is valuable, so they may not be willing to spend much time with new investors. Busy agents do not want to waste their time with a beginning investor making frivolous offers that don't get accepted. In a strong market, they can work with plenty of qualified conventional homebuyers. They don't need to deal with creative offers and nothing-down, pie-in-the-sky promises.

While this view does not always represent reality, it is how most agents think. As a beginner, you will get discouraged dealing with a buyer's agent who possesses this attitude, so make sure you approach your agent in the right way.

- Dress nicely. You want to look "money."
- Be respectful of the agent's time. For example, ask the agent to have an assistant fax or e-mail you the listings you are looking for.
- Drive by the properties you are interested in before asking the agent to show you the inside of each property.
- Don't come off as a hotshot, but do let the agent know you intend to buy more than one property and can offer repeat business. If you intend to sell the property retail, offer the agent the listing (and, of course, ask for a discount on the fee for this listing).

MORTGAGE BROKERS

Mortgage companies spend thousands of dollars every week for advertisements and telemarketers to generate leads. They often receive hundreds of dead leads from people in distress with no equity and no ability to qualify for a new loan. Contact some local brokers and offer to pay them for these names. Many of these borrowers are behind in their loan payments and may be facing foreclosure. This information is invaluable, because it is not made public until the lender commences foreclosure.

These borrowers may have little choice but to deal with you. But don't take advantage of them, because doing so will only hurt you in the end. Make a deal that is profitable for you, but be fair.

BANK-OWNED PROPERTIES

Properties that are foreclosed by a bank are called REOs (short for real estate owned). Contact your local banks and ask for the REO department. Let them know you buy properties. Some may have special financing available for these properties. It is not easy to establish relationships with these banks. However, once you reach the right people and establish yourself as a serious investor, they will call you with deals.

FARMING THE NEIGHBORHOODS

Successful real estate agents utilize a technique called "farming" to increase their business activity. They pick a neighborhood or two and focus their marketing efforts within that area. You should try the same technique. Start with a neighborhood that is relatively convenient for you.

Drive the Area

Spend a few weekends driving around the area. At first, your goal is to learn about the area, the style of houses, and the average prices. Over time, you may expand your farm area, but stay within areas that contain the type of homes you plan to purchase. It is not necessary to begin your investment career by learning every square mile of a large metropolitan area, but it is important to learn the value of typical homes in your target areas. This knowledge will enable you to make quick decisions about whether a particular prospect is a bargain.

Attend Open Houses

Visit open houses and for-sale-by-owner (FSBO) properties on weekends. Speak directly with the owners and their agents. Pass out your business cards. Make friends. Word of mouth and referrals are a big part of any business. (See the discussion later in this chapter.) Take a good look at the property and its physical features. After going to a couple dozen open houses in the neighborhood, you will get to know the value of the properties and the different styles of houses.

Look for Ugly and Vacant Properties

While you are driving around neighborhoods, look for vacant, ugly houses. How can you tell if a house is vacant? Look in the window! Of course, you should use a fair amount of discretion; this practice may get you shot, bitten by a dog, or arrested. First look for the obvious signs of vacancy: overgrown grass, no window shades, boarded windows, newspapers, garbage, mail piled up, etc. If you are not certain whether the property is vacant, knock on the door. If the owner answers, be polite and respectful and ask if he or she is interested in selling. In many cases, the home may be a rental property, so ask the occupants for the name and telephone number of the owner. Obviously, you should not visit these properties alone, especially at night.

If the property is vacant, ask the neighbors if they know the owner. Most neighbors are helpful, for they know ugly houses hurt their own property values. In addition, ask the mail carrier, who knows all of the empty houses on the block. Leave a business card and write down the address of the ugly or vacant property. When you get home, look up the name and address of the owner. Finding the owner of a vacant house can be difficult, which is why the persistent people who find the information make the most money. To determine the name of the owner, call your local tax assessor's office or look up the deed recorded with the county land records.

Contacting the owner takes a little more digging. Try speaking with the neighbors or asking the post office for a copy of a change-of-address form on file for the property. Online services such as http://www.infousa.com will search public databases, such as the Driver's License Bureau and the Department of Motor Vehicles, for a small fee.

Some cities, towns, and counties will tag a house with code violations. This is often a sign of a neglected or vacant property. Ask your city if you can obtain a list of such properties or find where this information is publicly recorded.

Use Direct Mail

Direct mail marketers are masters at working the numbers game. They mail postcards, flyers, brochures, and catalogs by the tens of thousands to prospective customers. Believe it or not, direct mail success is about 1 percent. That means a 99 percent failure rate! Here's a little secret: you can get filthy rich on a 1 percent success rate in direct mail.

Consider that a typical subdivision may have more than a thousand homes. If you were able to make $35,000 flipping 1 percent (ten homes) in that subdivision each year, you could operate a good little side business. Expand your efforts into five areas, and you have a very nice living.

Postcards are the cheapest and most effective way to cover a neighborhood. Go to the post office and buy a couple thousand postcards. Take them to a printer and have a simple message printed on the postcard, such as "We Buy Houses." (See sample ads in Appendix B.) You can also do the entire process online at http://www.USPS.gov. Don't expect to get all of the calls at once;

sometimes people call months after receiving your cards. Try mailing to the same people two or three times a year. You may get as many calls the second or third time around.

Marketing Works!

We bought a house at a nearly 50 percent discount from a man who called us. He had one foot out the door and was moving to another state. When we visited his house, he had a postcard on his refrigerator from us. We asked, "How long ago did we send that card to you?" He replied, "I got that postcard a year ago, but I've been waiting for my job transfer to go through."

PROMOTE YOURSELF

In addition to sending postcards, blanket the neighborhoods you choose with other marketing materials such as flyers and door hangers. When funds become available, consider more aggressive advertising, such as bus stop benches and supermarket shopping carts. When homeowners in the area are thinking of selling, they may call you before listing their property with an agent. By saving these people a real estate commission, you may be halfway to your desired purchase discount.

Distributing Flyers and Door Hangers

Don't spend your time passing out flyers and door hangers; rather, hire kids to do it for you. Go back and check to see if the job is done properly before you pay them. Instruct them not to place anything inside a mailbox; rather, put materials inside a screen door or fence, so as not to run afoul of postal regulations.

Door hangers are more expensive than flyers, but they are easier to distribute.

Carry door hangers and flyers in your car when you cruise neighborhoods. Whenever you see people in their yards or a for-sale-by-owner sign, stop and talk with the owners, then hand them a flyer.

Drive Around with Magnetic Car Signs

You can get magnetic signs to place on your car, truck, or minivan, making it a traveling billboard. We've seen entire vans and trucks with "We Buy Houses" all over them. These investors may deduct the entire vehicle as a marketing expense on their income taxes.

Share Expenses

Other unrelated businesses may be marketing their products or services in the same neighborhood using the same advertising means. Offer to split the expense to share your message. For example, if a pizzeria is distributing single-sided flyers, offer to pay for the printing if your message can appear on the back of the flyer. Also, check with local companies that send coupon mailers in bulk. It is much cheaper to mail information when multiple advertisers are involved.

Use Targeted Direct Mail

Earlier, we talked about directing a blind mailing to a targeted area. Rather than a blind mailing, try mailing to specific lists, such as:

- Out-of-state owners (these could be motivated landlords or job transferees),

- Homeowners with poor credit,
- People with federal tax liens, and
- People in foreclosure or bankruptcy within the past year (they may have been bailed out but still be in financial distress).

The names of these people can be purchased from a mailing list broker. Look in your local phone book under "Mailing List Companies." You should expect to pay 10 to 30 cents per name. In addition, keep a running list of the vacant houses, people who call on your ads, and other leads. Mail postcards to these people on a regular basis.

Color and Style of the Message

Many studies have been conducted by marketing companies to determine the most effective color, size, and wording of marketing pieces. In other words, what makes people tick? While this information is somewhat useful, don't get caught up in it—the most important part of marketing is repetition. Keep sending the mail until the recipients ask to be taken off your list or a postcard comes back marked "deceased," then find out who the heirs of the estate are. (See the following section.)

PROBATE ESTATES

Every year, countless people die owning real estate in your city. Often, these properties are in a state of disrepair, because the owners neglected them during their final years or because they sat vacant after their death. When someone dies with real estate in his or her name, the ownership does not automatically vest in the heirs of the deceased's estate. The deceased's will must be processed through a court proceeding known as probate. The probate proceeding can take as much as a year or more in some areas, depending on the backlog of court cases, the amount of the deceased's assets, and the battling between the heirs for their share of the estate. The typical heirs to an estate are no different than the average person; they have no experience in fixing or selling real estate. If the heirs have no emotional attachment to the property, they will be eager for the administrator of the estate to liquidate the property quickly, so they can receive their inheritance in cash.

The easiest place to find probate properties is in the newspaper. The obituaries can be cross-referenced with real estate records in your county. If your county tax assessor has free online listings of properties, run the names of the deceased through the database to find a match. Once you have a match, contact the local probate court to find out the name of the administrator of the estate. Even though particular situations may not present a deal for you, administrators can keep your name on file in case they are the administrator of other estates.

GETTING REFERRALS

As an individual you can cover only a limited amount of ground looking for bargain properties. Because your greatest profit is made at the purchase end of a transaction, it makes sense to enlist others to help you find deals. In fact, you will find that after a few years in the real estate business, your greatest source of deals will be from referrals.

Get a Great Business Card

Get a nice business card. No, get a really nice business card. Don't be cheap and use the basic white ones from Office Depot, and don't even think about making one on your computer. When you are dealing with a $200,000 asset, look professional. Don't be shy about spending $100 or more on your business cards.

Your card should be double-sided, with a complete message about what you do. (See Appendix B for sample business cards.) Your business should have a catchy name that tells what you do. CTM Investments tells people nothing, but Real Estate Solutions, Inc. tells a lot more. In addition, form a corporation for your business as soon as possible. (See Chapter 12.)

Start with People You Know

Pass out your business cards to everyone you know, including business contacts. Let them know you are interested, hand them your card, then ask, "Can you think of anyone you know who may have a run-down property?" The best salespeople always use this technique—you should, too.

Others in Your Farm Neighborhoods

Look for other people who are out working in your target neighborhoods each day. Mail carriers, delivery people, contractors, insurance agents, city building and zoning inspectors, carpenters, and painters all make excellent scouts. Introduce yourself to these people and explain that you are looking for run-down, deserted, and ugly properties.

Enlist Scouts

You may start out in this business as a scout, but you will soon be a dealer or a retailer in need of a scout or two. You can offer people a referral fee for information leading to a property you purchase. This amount can be anything from $500 to $1,000, depending on how good the deal is. A friend who just stumbled across information about properties will be happy to comply. If you are looking for real scouts, however, it will be difficult to keep them motivated if they only get paid when you buy a property.

Unfortunately, most beginners at any sales job quit after a few weeks, because they lack the mental discipline to stick it out until their first commission check comes. Scouts are no different, so you need to set up a modified payment structure to keep them interested. For example, you can pay $20 for each ugly, vacant house they find. The information should include a photograph of the house, the complete address, the owner's name, and information about the owner's distress (such as foreclosure, bankruptcy, divorce, etc.). You can also give them a couple hundred dollars as a bonus after you purchase the property.

FORECLOSURE PROPERTIES

Chasing foreclosures is slang for following properties through the foreclosure process while attempting to entice the owners to sell. Foreclosure properties can be the best or the most frustrating source of leads. The information is public, so every seminar junkie in town is competing with you. To work the foreclosure market successfully, you must understand how the foreclosure process works.

Foreclosure is the legal process of the mortgage holder taking the collateral for a promissory note in default. The process is slightly different from state to state, but there are basically two types of foreclosure: judicial and nonjudicial. In mortgage states, judicial foreclosure is commonly used, while in deed-of-trust states, nonjudicial foreclosure is the most common. Most states permit both types of proceedings, but standard practice in most states is to use exclusively one method or the other. (You can find a complete summary of each state's foreclosure rules in Appendix D.)

Judicial Foreclosure

Judicial foreclosure is a lawsuit that the lender (mortgagee) brings against the borrower (mortgagor) to get the property. About half of the states use judicial foreclosure. Like all lawsuits, foreclosure starts with a summons and a complaint served upon the borrower and any other parties with inferior rights in the property. (Remember, all junior liens, including tenancies, are wiped out by the foreclosure.)

If the borrower does not file an answer to the lawsuit, the lender gets a judgment by default. A referee is then appointed by the court to compute the total amount (including interest and attorney's fees) that is due. The lender then must advertise a notice of sale in the newspaper for four to six weeks. If the total amount due is not paid, the referee conducts a public sale on the courthouse steps. The entire process can take as little as 3 months and as many as 12 months depending on the volume of court cases in that county.

The sale is conducted like an auction, because the property goes to the highest bidder. Unless significant equity is in the property, the only bidder at the sale will be a representative of the lender. The lender can bid up to the amount it is owed, without actually having to come up with cash out of pocket to purchase the property.

If the proceeds from the sale are insufficient to satisfy the amount owed to the lender, the lender may be entitled to a deficiency judgment against the borrower and anyone else who guaranteed the loan. Some states (e.g., California) prohibit a lender from obtaining a deficiency judgment against a borrower.

Nonjudicial Foreclosure

Many states permit a lender to foreclose without a lawsuit, using what is commonly called a power of sale. Rather than a mortgage, the borrower (grantor) gives a deed of trust to a trustee to hold for the lender (beneficiary). Upon default, the lender simply files a notice of default and a notice of sale, which is published in the newspaper. The entire process generally takes about 90 days. The borrower usually has a right of redemption after the sale. (See the following section on redemption rights.) In some states, mortgages also contain a power of sale.

Strict Foreclosure

A few states permit strict foreclosure, which does not require a sale. When the proceeding is started, the borrower has a certain amount of time to pay what is owed. Once that date has passed, title reverts to the lender.

Reinstating the Loan

Many states permit a borrower to "cure the loan" before the date of sale. This process simply requires paying the amount in arrears, plus interest and attorney's fees. It is certainly more desirable for a defaulting borrower to reinstate a loan rather than pay off the entire principal balance. Most deed-of-trust states permit the borrower to reinstate the loan before the sale.

Redemption Rights

Some states give a borrower the right to redeem the amount owed and get title to the property back after the sale. The length of the redemption period varies from state to state. Obtaining a deed from the owner during the redemption period gives you the right to redeem the property.

Deed from the Owner

The easiest way to deal with a foreclosure is to get the owner to deed you the property. Once you have the deed to the property, you are the owner. You can now try to negotiate a discount on the amount owed to the foreclosing lender. Many lenders will not deal with you unless you have written permission from the owner, because releasing such information may violate Fair Credit Reporting Laws. It is a good idea to get a written authorization or a power of attorney from the seller along with the deed. Check with your state law for the proper form.

The best way to get in touch with the owners is to knock on their door. This is not only gutsy, it is risky. You may be dealing with a bitter, belligerent person. More than likely, you will be dealing with people who are not being honest with themselves about the situation. Don't try to bully the sellers into giving you the deed. Just let them know you are available, give them your business card, and check back from time to time. The more you follow up, the greater the chance that you will make a deal. At some point, the sellers in foreclosure will face reality, and they will usually sell to the first person who comes banging on their door. The more you stay in touch, the greater the chance that you will be that person. (Note: Before you get a deed from a seller in foreclosure, you may need to have a written contract with certain disclosures mandated by the law of the state. At this printing, those states include California, Maryland, Minnesota, and Missouri; several more states are considering similar legislation.)

GETTING PAID *NOT* TO BUY

Because many people in foreclosure are deluded into thinking they have options other than selling to you, offer the buyout contract. In essence, your written contract will give the sellers the right to cancel if they obtain a written offer better than yours before your closing date. That buyout fee is negotiable, but make sure it is enough to make it worth your while.

Visit your local courthouse to find names of property owners in foreclosure. Better yet, subscribe to one of the local foreclosure listing services. These companies gather this information each week and sell it for a reasonable fee, saving you a great deal of time. The information you want to buy is the list of people in foreclosure, not properties that have been already foreclosed and have been taken back by the bank. Check your local phone book and ask other investors in your area which services are reputable.

Buy Property at the Sale

In a foreclosure, there is a public sale of the property in all but strict foreclosure states. Contact your local courthouse and ask where this sale will happen. Visit a few sales to watch the action before engaging in a bid. Don't be surprised if no one bids but the foreclosing lender. Most properties in foreclosure don't have enough equity to justify a bid from an investor.

To buy at the foreclosure sale, you must bring certified funds for a portion of the bid price. The balance is usually due within a few weeks of the sale. You need some experience to buy properties at auction, so consider holding off until you have a few deals under your belt or have a partner who can show you the ropes.

Buy the Liens

At any time during the foreclosure process, you can buy the mortgage from the lender and finish the foreclosure. If the first mortgage is relatively small compared to the value of the property, it may be worthwhile to buy it. This method, of course, requires a lot of capital and experience.

In states that have a redemption period, many of the deals happen during that time. Remember that redemption is the right to purchase the property out of the foreclosure for the entire balance owed. The highest right of redemption is from the owner, borrower, or guarantor on the note. If none of these people redeem, the junior lien holders, who are in danger of being wiped out by the foreclosing senior lien holder, can redeem the property. Thus, if there are two mortgages on the property and the first mortgage holder is foreclosing, the second mortgage holder can redeem the property by paying what is owed on the first mortgage, plus late fees, court costs, and interest. The second mortgage holder then becomes the owner of the property. This process is technical and tricky, and it often attracts crooks and scam artists who create phony liens in an attempt to redeem the property.

GOVERNMENT-OWNED PROPERTIES

The federal government becomes the owner of tens of thousands of properties each year. Many can be purchased at good discounts, if you know how to find them.

FHA/VA "Repos"

Certain loan programs are guaranteed or insured by the federal government. The Federal Housing Administration (FHA), which operates under the Department of Housing and Urban Development (HUD), insures certain loans targeted at first-time homebuyers in lower income neighborhoods. The Veterans Administration (VA) guarantees similar loans for military personnel and their families. When these loans are in default, the government ends up with the properties.

Most of these properties are listed and sold through real estate agents. The property is first offered to potential owner-occupants in a bid process. When no suitable owner-occupant is found, the properties go on an extended listing, which is offered to everyone, including investors. You can place a bid on these properties with as little as $1,000 as earnest money, and, if your bid is accepted, you have about 60 days to close. You can even extend that date a few weeks by paying a reasonable fee.

The bidding process is difficult, and you need a savvy real estate agent to help you along. As you may have guessed, the great thing about the HUD/VA process is that you have a long time to close and are only required to risk $1,000 in earnest money. However, the HUD/VA contract has no "weasel clauses," so you will lose your earnest money if you fail to close.

Furthermore, the HUD/VA contract is not assignable, so you have to do a double closing to flip the property to another investor. If you get the property at the right price, 60 days is more than enough time to make things happen.

KEY POINTS TO REMEMBER

- Find a motivated seller, and you find a bargain property
- Learn how to farm neighborhoods
- Employ multiple marketing approaches
- Use your business card and contacts to get referral business
- Learn how to work the foreclosure business

4

ANALYZING A GOOD DEAL

It takes experience to recognize a profitable deal. Of course, experience usually comes from making lots of mistakes. Use this book to learn from our mistakes, so you don't lose money the hard way. Be aware of local and regional market trends, but do not be paralyzed by these trends. The concept of flipping properties works in every market, in every city, whether the market is hot or in the pits.

PICK THE RIGHT NEIGHBORHOODS

You can flip houses in any neighborhood, but start with the low- to middle-priced areas that are 15 to 50 years old. Don't buy in gang-ridden, high-crime areas at first, for your market for resale is very small. Buy in working-class areas where housing is affordable and desirable. Beware of the so-called median price or some figure that real estate agents use. This figure may be skewed by higher-priced, newly constructed homes around the corner. Furthermore, stay with the populated areas that are in high demand. You can make a profit in other areas, but this approach takes more experience and involves more risk. As a beginner, follow these guidelines, and you can't go wrong.

Starter Homes

Concentrate on purchasing starter homes at first. These homes are the least expensive single-family homes (and possibly condominiums) in each area. Usually they will be two- or three-bedroom ranch-style houses. If possible, choose an area close to where you live. Staying close to home means you know the neighborhood and its current trends. The neighborhood does not need to be in a location where you would choose to live, but it should not be in a slum, either. If you are not sure about an area, check the local police departments for available crime statistics. Other resources include the local chamber of commerce, planning department, real estate agents, and census reports. You should also subscribe to (and read!) local and regional newspapers.

PICK THE RIGHT KIND OF HOUSES

Choose houses that are consistent with the neighborhood. For example, don't buy one-bedroom houses unless there are several in the area. If you are in a warm, humid climate, make sure the house has air conditioning. If every house in the area has two bedrooms, don't buy a five-bedroom home; it may be overpriced for the area. You are always better off buying the cheapest house in a better neighborhood than the highest-priced house in a poor neighborhood.

Functional Obsolescence

Be wary of poorly designed houses. It is okay to buy a house that needs work or remodeling, but don't buy houses with basic design problems, such as five bedrooms and only one bath and no tub. Beware of the odd-man-out house on the block. For example, if every house has a garage and the subject house does not, you could have a problem when you try to sell it. If each house on the block was built in the 1950s, don't buy the old farmhouse that was built in 1890, unless you plan on demolishing it. Finally, keep in mind that the house may eventually be purchased by a retail buyer with FHA or VA financing (the Federal Housing Administration insures FHA loans and the Department of Veterans Affairs guarantees VA loans). The house must conform to strict guidelines for the government to guarantee the loan. You can learn what these guidelines are by contacting your local HUD or VA office and by talking to appraisers in your area.

ESTABLISH VALUE

It is extremely important to establish the value of a property before making an offer. Base your offer on what the house will sell for after necessary repairs. Remember to learn the area first, and buy in your "farm area" when possible. (See Chapter 3.) Always take a conservative approach until you gain experience in dealing in a particular market. Start with a few neighborhoods within a subdivision that contain similar houses, because dealing with similar houses makes price comparisons much easier.

Use Professional Help

An expensive but accurate way to determine the value of a home is to hire a licensed appraiser. The appraisal will cost you around $300. This amount is cheap compared to what you could potentially lose, but appraisals can be costly if you are making multiple offers. It may be worthwhile to pay an appraiser on your first purchases to verify your assumptions of value (but not until you have the properties under contract). In addition, follow appraisers as they inspect the properties and ask a lot of questions to learn how they arrive at their figures.

Basically, licensed appraisers look at the three most similar houses in the vicinity that have sold recently. They then compare square footage and other attributes. (See the sample appraisal form in Appendix C.) The number of bedrooms and baths, age of the property, improvements, physical condition, and the presence of a garage will affect the price, but square footage is usually the most important factor. As you might expect, there are exceptions to this rule. For example, the style of house, its location and proximity to main roads, and whether it has a view or beach access will greatly affect the value. Of course, you probably will not be flipping many beachfront properties. For the most part, however, if you leave these issues aside, square footage, number of bedrooms and baths, and physical condition are the most relevant factors.

Doing Your Own Appraisal

Doing an appraisal yourself is not that difficult. You start by accessing information about houses sold recently. Until now, access to this information was limited to licensed real estate agents through the Multiple Listing Service (MLS). In today's Information Age, this data is available through various channels such as

Value versus Appeal

There are certain items you can fix that will not raise the value of the property but will change its appeal. For example, renovating a kitchen should not affect the appraisal value of a property, because it doesn't add living space or functionality. But if the kitchen looks horrid, the house is not in marketable condition and will attract fewer buyers, take longer to sell, and command a lower price.

Also, keep in mind that bedrooms and baths on the main level add more value than bedrooms and baths in a basement or attic. Thus, while a finished basement may add some appeal and functionality, it may not raise the appraisal value of the property by much. Whether it is worth finishing a basement depends on a lot of factors, including what is customary for the area. For example, a new ranch house with a walkout from the basement will have much more value with a finished basement than a three-story, 100-year-old Victorian.

the county tax assessor, Internet Web sites, or paid providers. (You will find a list of these sites in Appendix E.)

Armed with information about properties sold in the area, you can drive by these houses and compare them with the subject property. You will not be able to see the inside, so you need to adjust your numbers a bit. Also, public records may have inaccurate information about square footage, additions, number of beds and baths, and basement versus above-ground living space. In addition, public records do not offer much detail, and the property may have been improved or expanded after it was built.

All of these variables aside, you can still assess the style of property, whether it has a garage, its general condition, and appearance. Only look at houses sold in the area within the past six months. Try to acquire information about the type of financing on the house, because terms can influence the sales price. For example, an owner-carry sale (one in which the seller takes all or part of the purchase price in the form of a note) at an inflated price should not be considered in your figures, because these prices tend to be artificially high.

Keep in mind that seasons affect sales prices. Most people prefer to buy in the summer when their children are out of school. Additionally, if you are in a resort area, prices may fluctuate drastically between the summer and the winter.

Comparable Sales

A practical but less accurate way to establish value is by asking a real estate agent for comparable sales or "comps." If the property is listed or you are using a buyer's agent, as described in Chapter 3, agents will gladly provide this information free of charge. Some listing agents will have prepared a written comparative market analysis (CMA) for the property. You cannot always rely on the MLS information about the inside, however, because agents' property descriptions tend to be exaggerated. Furthermore, the information on the comparable properties that agents give you may only contain the ones they want you to see. The lesson here is to never rely solely on an agent's comps or CMAs but do your own due diligence.

If the property was refinanced in the past year or so, take a look at the seller's appraisal. Keep in mind that some appraisers will inflate the value of the property if they are in close with the mortgage broker handling the refinancing. This practice is legal within limits, because the appraiser is required to determine property value based on certain guidelines. Sellers want a high appraisal, so their appraiser will employ the highest comps. A person fighting a high property tax assessment can instruct the appraiser to find low (while still conforming) comparable sales.

A House Is Often Its Own Best "Comp"

If a particular house has been listed on the local MLS longer than the average listing period, chances are the house is priced too high. A seller may show you an appraisal from a refinance process six months ago, showing a price even higher than that. Don't be fooled—the market will determine what a house is worth. Thus, if a house is appraised for $200,000 and has been sitting on the market for six months, there's an obvious conclusion—it's not worth $200,000. In short, be careful of appraisals that don't jibe with reality.

WHAT IS A GOOD DEAL?

No one formula works in every neighborhood and in every market. It takes experience to recognize the potential in a real estate transaction. The catch-22 is that lack of experience will make it harder to recognize a good deal. More often than not, investors pay too much for properties. People who buy for speculation often get hurt financially, because they are depending on factors beyond their control, such as the market, the neighborhood, favorable zoning, or other long-term factors. As a property flipper, do not be concerned with factors beyond your control. To make your profit when you purchase, buy it right!

This may sound redundant, but don't make the mistake of paying too much for a property. Believe it or not, most investors know what they want to pay for a property but are afraid to ask. They are also afraid that the seller will be offended and refuse to negotiate further. A seller will only be offended if you ask in the wrong way.

Pay Full Price and Still Profit—"Speculative Flipping"

In Chapter 1, we discouraged your acting as a real estate spec-
ulator. However, as a dealer, you can flip properties to speculators.
In certain inner-city neighborhoods, developers and speculators
are willing to pay full price and more for properties—not for the
house, but for the land value. Often homeowners in the path of a
new development are stubborn and refuse to sell to these developers and speculators. These homeowners may, however, sell to you,
simply because they like you! Thus, you can sign a purchase contract for full price and flip it to a developer for more money.

In some areas of the country, new developments are sold out
before the houses are built. This lack of supply may increase the
value of properties in the development by as much as 20 percent
by the time all the houses are finished. With as little as $1,000
down, you can sign a contract with the developer to purchase a
home before it is built. By the time the house is complete, you
can find an owner-occupant to buy the house from you in a double closing. This is one of the few times you will act as both a
dealer and retailer. Speculative flipping is just that—speculative.
With speculation comes greater risk, and beginners should avoid
doing it.

Presumably, you will start out as a scout or dealer, so you need
to establish the wholesale price for a property. As with any other
business, there is a wholesale price and a retail price. Find out
what kind of discount the retailers are looking for and you have a
starting point. For example, a retailer may be willing to pay 80
percent of the property's market value. Subtract from that discounted price the estimated cost of repairs (as we will discuss in
Chapter 9), leaving a healthy margin for error. Then subtract
your profit in the deal. Your profit may be anywhere from $1,000
to $5,000, depending on the price of the property and your mar-
ketplace.

Don't Be Greedy

When figuring in your profit, don't expect too much. Many amateur and some experienced, albeit foolish, investors expect more profit than they deserve out of a deal. Be realistic. If you want to sell a property quickly to another investor who will do a lot of work, you can't expect to make as much as the investor.

Add in Your Profit

The corollary to *don't be greedy* is to remember to make your offer with two investors in mind. A lot of beginning dealers forget that there must be enough profit in the deal for both themselves and the retailer to make money. Thus, you must offer the seller the wholesale price minus your anticipated profit.

Let's summarize the price you are looking for as a dealer:

	Retail price	Established by appraisal and/or comps
× 0.8	Discount	Established by local property retailers
–	Repairs	Estimated conservatively
–	Your fee	$1,000 to $5,000
=	Your purchase price	$ _____

The Retailer's Bid

It is relatively easy to find a starting point as a dealer; simply ask the retailer what he or she is willing to pay you. Thus, being a retailer takes a little more experience in estimating the following factors:

- market value of the property after resale;
- acquisition and financing costs;

- labor and material costs (include cost overruns);
- time required to complete repairs, weather factors, and availability of labor;
- estimated time on the market;
- time involved for supervising construction; and
- real estate agent commissions and other sales costs.

No magic formula works in every market, in every neighborhood, for every house. In our market (Denver, Colorado), the market is rather flat, so we buy properties at 80 percent of the market value or less. In hot markets, you can pay as high as 90 percent and still profit, because the property is likely to appreciate another 5 to 10 percent by the time you have rehabbed it. You don't need to be in an up market to make a profit flipping properties, but it is important to know where your market currently is and where it is going.

Our recommendation is to flip a few properties first, then review the numbers on those properties with the retailers who sold them to the owner-occupants. After reviewing a dozen or so deals with several retailers, you will get a feel for what kind of discount is necessary.

After establishing the retail price, the appropriate discount, repairs, and your profit, you finally arrive at your offering price, right? Wrong! This price is the maximum you can afford to pay. Leave enough room in the equation for the seller's counter-offer. This brings us to the next topic: negotiating!

Don't Be the "Greater Fool"

Flipping is a hot topic these days, so plenty of unscrupulous people are trying to make money on the "greater fool" theory. Investors are buying properties and flipping them to inexperienced investors by telling them, "This is a wholesale deal," when they know it is a marginal deal. New investors end up with properties they have paid nearly full price for, and they have no way to get rid of them. This commonly happens when properties are located away from the new investor's hometown and the newbie relies on professional advice from real estate brokers and developers.

Some operators even charge you to get into an exclusive "network" in which they supply you with unlimited deals. The idea that an unlimited number of wholesale deals is waiting for someone to find is specious at best. Finding really good deals is not easy—it takes a lot of work and a bit of good luck. Approach anyone who promises a shortcut to that process with a great deal of skepticism. A sucker is born every minute—don't be one of them.

KEY POINTS TO REMEMBER

- Pick the right neighborhoods

- Learn how to establish value

- Find out what other investors are willing to pay for properties and find deals that suit their needs

5

THE ART OF NEGOTIATING THE DEAL

Negotiating the right price and/or terms for your properties is the most important part of the profit-making process. Many people are either afraid to negotiate or inept at the negotiating process. Other so-called investors pay too much for a property and then are left with no way to make a profit other than the "greater fool" theory. Learn to negotiate a good purchase price quickly, or you will face a tough road ahead.

DEAL ONLY WITH MOTIVATED SELLERS

The biggest mistake you can make is negotiating with someone who is not highly motivated to sell. Once in a while, you will run across the "garage sale" seller—that is, someone without a clue about the value of the property. These opportunities are rare, and pursuing them will not make you a living. Rather than taking advantage of ignorant people, deal with people who *need* and *want* to sell quickly.

Find Out What the Seller Wants

Many novice investors spend countless hours researching the property, the needed repairs, the taxes, and other information without first finding out the seller's motivation. This mistake relates to the rule about never dealing with unmotivated people. Once you have established that someone is motivated, dig deeper. Find out exactly what makes this seller tick. Why does this person need to sell? By when does the individual need to sell? Is price more important than terms? What will the seller do with the proceeds? You need to get these questions answered before you even consider making an offer—even before going to see the property. Instead of jumping right in with tough questions that may offend the seller, start by asking a few questions about the property. Don't be too concerned with the physical aspects of the property when talking with a seller on the phone. Your goal is to determine whether the seller is motivated enough to make you a deal. Talk about the weather, sports teams, how much you hate politicians, etc. When you sense the seller is opening up a bit, ask the following questions:

- "Why are you selling?"
- "How long have you owned the property?"
- "What did you pay for it when you bought it?"
- "When do you need to sell it by?"
- "Have you listed it with a real estate agent? Why/Why not?"
- "What are your plans after you sell?"
- "After paying all the closing costs and paying off your loan, what is the minimum amount of cash you need in your pocket?
- "What will you do with the proceeds from the sale of your house?"
- "If I were to close in a week and pay all cash, what is the very best you can do in terms of price?"

Continue to develop your phone skills and try experimenting with new questions. You need to communicate in a way that works with your personality. No one can tell you all the perfect things to say for each situation. Just be yourself; develop rapport and zone in on what the seller needs. The best salespeople are those who find what their customers need and present their product in a way that fulfills those needs. Successful investors are essentially problem solvers. Problem solvers are among the highest-paid individuals in the world. The problems homeowners face may seem insurmountable to them. With experience and practice, however, you will learn many approaches to solving their problems. It is just a matter of time until you, the investor, will earn a profit while helping homeowners solve their problems in an ethical way.

Just for practice, record your telephone conversations with motivated sellers (as long as it's not illegal in your state). Use these recordings to improve your sales pitch. Track your results, and you will soon find an effective approach for making your calls.

Let the Seller Make You an Offer

Most novice investors make the foolish mistake of always making the first offer. While in some circumstances, this approach may be appropriate or desirable, if your offer is too low, the seller may be offended. Let the seller make the first move. "Mr. Seller, what is the best deal you can offer me on this property?" This statement puts the pressure on the seller, who may be afraid of driving you away by asking too much. Whatever your prospect offers, you ask him or her to do better. Henry Kissinger was the master of this technique. He would routinely send back proposals without reading them, saying, "You can do better." Get the seller to go as low as possible, then negotiate from there.

Leave Yourself Room to Negotiate

Once you get a contract accepted at the price you like, it may still be too much. Leave room for error or for things you overlooked. Always have an inspection clause in your contract that allows you to dicker with the seller and to renegotiate if necessary. (See Chapter 6.) Please understand—we are not advocating that you beat up people after you agree on a price. However, sometimes you will discover problems with the property that were unknown to either party or that the seller conveniently forgot to tell you about. As a real estate agent friend used to say, "All sellers are storytellers!"

PRICE ISN'T EVERYTHING

As discussed previously, it is essential to know what motivates a seller. Some sellers want the highest price, but many just want their problems solved quickly. That's where you can truly help. Here are some ways to do so.

Offer a Fast Closing

Offering a fast closing with few contingencies will often perk up the seller's ears. If the seller says, "A real estate agent told me the property is worth more," you respond with, "Does the real estate agent have a buyer ready to close next week?" Sometimes offering a contract with no contingencies is your strongest offer, especially when dealing with real estate agents. (See a later section in this chapter.) Of course, a real estate contract with no contingencies is risky, because you will lose your earnest money deposit if you fail to purchase the property. (See Chapter 6.)

Purchase "Subject to" the Existing Mortgage

When retailers quote you the appropriate discount they want, they are including the cost of financing the property. Most retailers use credit lines and/or conventional bank financing to purchase properties. These loans have certain costs associated with them, which reduce the net profit in the deal. Whether you are a dealer or a retailer, you can save money by avoiding these new loan costs, thus offering the seller a higher price (or more net cash in the seller's pocket).

Chances are, the seller has an existing loan on the property. Offer the seller the cash difference between the purchase price and the seller's loan balance. At the closing, you take the title subject to the existing mortgage. (See Chapter 2 for a discussion on "subject to" transfers.) You make the monthly payments directly to the seller's lender and pay off the balance of the mortgage when the property is sold to the retail buyer. Even if you are buying the property with "subject to" conditions as a dealer, you can pass these savings on to the retailer who buys the property from you. Another benefit of the "subject to" transaction is that it allows you to close without a third-party lender, which translates to a faster closing.

The Split-Funded Sale

A seller you are negotiating with may own a property outright or may have a very small mortgage. Thus, the seller may receive more cash from closing than needed (which you have already established by asking good questions). If this is the case, offer to split-fund the purchase price. Split-funding means you will pay the seller "some now, some later." Offer to pay 20 percent at closing, followed by another 20 percent in 60 days, and the balance in

6 months. Be creative with your offers and conserve your cash whenever possible.

Multiple Offers

When you make an offer, the seller has two choices: take it or leave it. When you make two alternative offers, the seller has more choices. For example, you can offer the seller all cash and a 30-day closing or a split-funded purchase that closes next week. In some cases, it doesn't even occur to the seller that he or she doesn't need to accept either offer!

If You Make a Concession, Get Something in Return

This strategy is one of the most underused in the negotiation game. If the seller asks for more money, you ask for more time. If the seller asks for a shorter closing date, you ask for the appliances. Never give a concession without getting something in return.

DEALING WITH REAL ESTATE AGENTS

Real estate agents have access to a valuable source of potential deals for the investor—the Multiple Listing Service (MLS). Unfortunately, real estate agents have a monopoly on this information, so they may be a necessary part of an investor's game plan.

Dealing with real estate agents can be difficult as an investor. Agents prefer homebuyers with cash for down payments. They also prefer to work with buyers who have good credit and conventional buying power. The agent's priority is getting a commission with as little hassle as possible. Most agents have never conducted a creative real estate transaction with an investor. These agents are not very receptive to unusual offers. Most agents equate a nothing-down offer with a buyer who is not serious.

Offer Reasonable Earnest Money

You cannot present an offer with a $50 earnest money deposit and expect an agent to take you seriously. Expect to pay at least $500 to $1,000 earnest money, depending on the purchase price, to get the agent's (and seller's) attention. Offer more earnest money when presenting an all-cash offer. If you are concerned with losing your earnest money, consider using a promissory note. (See Chapter 6.)

Offer a Short Closing Date

Another way to get an agent's attention is to offer a fast closing. Nothing makes an agent more excited than the thought of a commission check in ten days. When deciding between two offers, the agent will usually advise the client to accept an offer with more earnest money and a faster closing over a higher-priced offer.

Present Creative Offers in Person

When you present an offer to an agent, the agent then presents it to the seller on your behalf. If you present a creative offer, the agent probably will not represent your offer to the seller in an enthusiastic fashion. As stated previously, agents do not like creative offers; they like conventional offers from solid buyers. If you want the owner to understand all the benefits of your offer, insist on personally presenting the offer to the seller.

Appeal to the Agent's Greed

Let's face it, real estate agents are in the game to make money, just like people in other businesses. If you offer agents an opportunity to make money out of the transaction, you will get their cooperation. If you present an offer that does not provide enough cash to pay the agent, then the agent has no reason to cooperate with you. For example, if you present a nothing-down offer on a listed property, how will the agent receive a commission? You must include a means to pay the agent, even if you pay out of your own pocket.

Do Your Own Comps

Sometimes you will deal with the opposite of an uncooperative agent—an overzealous agent. Be suspicious of agents who tell you what a deal you are getting on a property. If it is such a good deal, why didn't they buy it? Do not trust them to determine the property's value. Do your own assessment of value. Remember, agents are looking out for their commission, not for your financial well-being.

Fax Preliminary Offers First

Technically speaking, all offers presented by agents must be made on state-approved contracts. But don't waste time filling out a contract offer until you have preliminary approval. Most agents are willing to present any written offer to the seller. Simply summarize your offer in writing and fax it to the listing agent. (See a sample fax offer form in Appendix C.) Once you have an oral approval, take the time to fill out a contract and deliver an earnest money check. Never put up earnest money until your offer is accepted. Fax the offer with a copy of an earnest money check with originals to be delivered "upon acceptance of contract."

Don't Be Bullied by Uncooperative Agents

Do not be afraid to stand up to an uncooperative agent. Some agents are unethical and will refuse to present your offer. These agents may lie, telling you that your offer was rejected when, in fact, it was never presented. If you suspect the listing agent is lying, go over that person's head to the managing broker of the office. If the managing broker is uncooperative, deal directly with the seller (unless, of course, you are also an agent). Be polite, but firm, and do not hesitate to report any unethical behavior to your state's agency responsible for regulating real estate agents.

KEY POINTS TO REMEMBER

- Only negotiate with motivated sellers
- Ask the right questions to determine the seller's level of motivation
- Negotiate a discount in price and/or a "subject to" deal
- Learn how to deal with real estate agents

6

PUTTING IT IN WRITING

Talk is cheap. Without a written agreement, you don't have a deal. At some point after negotiating with a seller (or buyer), you need to get things in writing. A well-written real estate agreement will save you a lot of headaches, arguments, and legal problems, so having good legal counsel review your deals and your business practices is important. However, your lawyer won't always be there when you need one, so you have to learn how to draft your own contracts. While the sample contracts found in Appendix C of this book are a good start, we advise you to review your contracts and processes with your local attorney.

BASIC CONTRACT PRINCIPLES

Real estate contracts are based on common contract principles, so it's important to understand the basics of contract law.

Offer, Counteroffer, and Acceptance

The process begins with an offer. A contract is formed when an offer is made and accepted. In most states, standardized contracts drafted in the form of offers are used by real estate agents and attorneys. The offer is usually signed by the buyer (the offeror) and contains all the material terms of a contract, with the exception of the seller's signature.

The basic building block of a contract is mutual agreement. The contract is not binding until the seller accepts, creating a meeting of the minds. An acceptance is made if the offeree (the seller, in this case) agrees to the exact terms of the offer. If the offer comes back to the offeror with changes, there is no binding contract but rather a counteroffer. Thus, if the seller signs the purchase contract but changes the closing date to five days sooner, there is no agreement. Furthermore, if the offer is not accepted in the time frame and manner set forth by the offeror, then there is no contract. For example, if the contract specifies that acceptance must be made by facsimile, an acceptance by telephone call or mail will not suffice.

Unilateral Contract versus Bilateral Contract

A real estate sales contract is a bilateral or two-way agreement. The seller agrees to sell, and the purchaser agrees to buy. Compare this agreement with an option: an option is a unilateral or one-way agreement by which the seller is obligated to sell, but the purchaser is not obligated to buy. On the other hand, if the purchaser on a bilateral contract refuses to buy, the purchaser can be held liable for damages.

A contract with a contingency is similar to an option. Many contracts contain contingencies (see the contingency section in this chapter), which, if not met, result in the termination of the contract. In essence, a bilateral contract with a contingency in favor of the purchaser turns a bilateral contract into an option because it gives the purchaser an out if they decide not to purchase the property. Though the two are not legally the same, an option and a bilateral purchase contract with a contingency yield the same practical results.

BASIC LEGAL REQUIREMENTS OF A REAL ESTATE CONTRACT

Several basic requirements must be present to make a real estate contract valid.

- *Mutual agreement.* As stated earlier, there must be a mutual agreement or a meeting of the minds.
- *In writing.* With few exceptions, a contract for purchase and sale of real estate must be in writing to be enforceable. Thus, if a buyer makes an offer in writing and the seller accepts orally and then backs out, the buyer is out of luck.
- *Identify the parties.* The contract must identify the parties. Although not legally required, a contract commonly sets forth full names and middle initials. (This helps the title company prepare the title commitment.) If one of the parties is a corporation, it should so state (e.g., North American Land Acquisitions, Inc., a Nevada corporation).
- *Identify the property.* The contract must identify the property. Although not required, a legal description should be included. A vague description such as "my lakefront home" may not be specific enough to create a binding contract.
- *Purchase price.* The contract must state the purchase price of the property or a reasonably ascertainable figure (e.g., "appraised value as determined by ABC Appraisers, Inc.").
- *Consideration.* A contract must have consideration to be enforceable. Consideration is the benefit, interest, or value

that induces a promise; it is the glue that binds a contract. The amount of consideration is not important, but rather whether there is consideration at all. It is common for a contract to read that, "Ten dollars and other good and valuable consideration has been paid and received." Consideration need not be cash; it can be property, a promissory note, or an agreement to perform services.

- *Signatures.* A contract must be signed to be enforceable. The party signing must be of legal age and sound mind. A notary's signature or witness is not required. A facsimile signature is usually acceptable, as long as the contract states that facsimile signatures are valid.

EARNEST MONEY

A buyer will usually put up earnest money to bind the contract and show seriousness as a buyer. Most sellers ask for the earnest money deposit, because they are afraid of tying up the property and rejecting other potential buyers.

How Much Earnest Money Is Necessary?

The law requires no specific amount of earnest money. In fact, if the transaction involves the buyer simply taking over a loan and the property has no equity, it may be appropriate for the seller to give the buyer consideration. When you are buying, you want to put down as little money as possible ($500 or less), though adding more will give your offer credibility. When selling, you should get as much as possible ($1,000 to $5,000). Of course, the amount of earnest money will depend on the motivation of the parties, the seller's representation by real estate professionals, the purchase price, and the length of time until closing.

If you are dealing with a seller represented by an agent, you may not be taken seriously with an offer that involves $100 earnest money. You should expect to put down at least 1 percent of the purchase price as earnest money or expect to get your offer laughed at. Also, when dealing directly with motivated sellers, the amount of earnest money you offer can often be a test of their motivation. Try verbally offering $100 earnest while negotiating and writing up the contract to see what response the seller gives you.

Should You "Pre-fill" the Contract?

Attorneys and real estate agents often "pre-fill" contracts before the parties meet. We think this is a mistake. If you show up with a pre-filled contract, the seller may get nervous and bail out on the deal. Instead, fill out the contract by hand in front of the seller as you negotiate each item. In sales circles, this is known as the "order form" close, commonly used by car salespersons.

Promissory Note

If you are afraid of losing your earnest money as a buyer, you may consider offering a promissory note as earnest money. A seller may be reluctant to accept a promissory note rather than cash, because if you default, the seller must sue you to collect on the note. As a compromise, you can structure the contract so the seller receives a promissory note as earnest money that is paid in full after the property is inspected but prior to closing.

Who Should Hold the Earnest Money?

A big issue for the parties is who should hold the earnest money deposit in escrow. Theoretically, the escrow agent (the person holding the earnest money) must release the funds to the seller if the buyer breaches and to the buyer if the contract is canceled. However, the escrow agent will not usually release the funds without the permission of both parties, even in the face of a clear breach or cancellation. Furthermore, if the escrow agent is the listing broker, the agent may side with the seller and not release the money. Listing brokers have an incentive to keep the earnest money, because their listing agreement usually gives them part of the forfeited earnest money deposit as a commission. The seller would obviously prefer to have the broker hold escrow, while the buyer would want a neutral or buyer-friendly title or escrow company to hold the earnest money.

CONTINGENCIES

As mentioned earlier, a contingency is a clause in a contract that must be satisfied for the contract to be complete. If the contingencies are not satisfied, the contract terminates, and the parties go their merry ways. The contract will usually provide that, in the event of termination, the buyer is entitled to a return of the earnest money.

Inspection Contingency

Most standard real estate contracts contain an inspection clause, which gives the buyer a certain amount of time to inspect the premises. After inspecting the premises, the buyer should provide the seller with a list of potential problems or defects and give the seller a chance to remedy these problems, adjust the purchase price, or choose to terminate the agreement. Most standard inspection clauses place the burden of inspecting and disapproving on the buyer. Thus, the buyer's failure to timely inspect and object will result in a waiver of this contingency. Used properly, the inspection clause will allow a buyer to terminate a contract that was signed hastily and later turns out to be a bad deal.

Inspection clauses can be written in a variety of ways. As the buyer, of course, you would prefer a more liberal, subjective approach, permitting you to perform the inspection without a licensed professional and disapprove of items in any manner you wish. However, you cannot use the inspection clause in an arbitrary fashion to cancel a purchase contract, for there is an implied duty of good faith on your part to deal fairly. For example, if you don't inspect the property or you inspect it briefly and raise minor objections, then walk away from the deal, you could be in breach of your contract.

Loan Approval Contingency

Virtually every standard real estate contract gives the buyer a contingency to find a loan to purchase the property. Once again, there's an implied duty of good faith here, so the buyer cannot simply sit back and say, "Oh well, I couldn't get a loan." The buyer is obligated to make reasonable efforts to apply to various lenders and comply with their demands for proof of employment, copies of tax returns, etc. The loan contingency will usually state a certain date by which the buyer must present the seller with a copy of a written loan commitment from the lender. If the deadline is not met, the seller can extend the deadline or the contract fails.

Marketable Title

The contract will usually provide that it is contingent upon proof of a marketable title by a certain date. The seller is usually required to provide the buyer a copy of a title report or a title commitment showing that the title is insurable. Even if the title report shows problems with the title, the contract is still in force if the seller can cure the problems before the closing and deliver a marketable title. For example, an existing mortgage lien or judgment is not fatal, because it can be satisfied by the seller from the proceeds at the closing.

BREACH OF CONTRACT

What happens when one party breaches the agreement? Breach of contract has many legal implications, but it is more important that you understand the practical side, for real estate litigation is usually a costly matter that should be avoided.

BUYER'S REMEDIES FOR BREACH

If the seller breaches the contract by failing to close the title, the buyer has three legal remedies:

1. Sue for specific performance
2. Sue for damages
3. Sue for return of the earnest money

Sue for Specific Performance

Specific performance is a remedy granted by a court, which forces the seller to sell to the buyer. If the property is unique and you feel like spending $10,000 in legal fees, then you will probably win the lawsuit if the seller refuses to close title. If the seller refused to close because he or she got "greedy" and found another buyer, you can record a copy of your contract or an affidavit (called a memorandum of agreement) in the public records. This will create a cloud on the title, which will alarm other buyers and title companies and may prevent the seller from closing with another buyer. Obviously, recording a contract or memorandum is a much more inexpensive and practical approach than suing. (You will find a sample Memorandum of Agreement form in Appendix C.)

Don't Get Sued for "Slander of Title"

Be mindful that if you record the memorandum without sufficient legal cause, you can be sued by the seller for "slander of title." We advise you to consider seeking legal counsel before filing such a document.

Sue for Damages

If the property was to be purchased at a discount or was intended to be resold for a profit, you may be able to sue for your loss of potential profit. Of course, loss of profit is difficult to prove, for it is not clear exactly at what price you could have sold the property, how long the sale would have taken, and how much the deal would have cost in repairs. Even if you could prove these factors through expert testimony, the lawsuit could cost you $10,000 in legal fees.

Sue for Return of the Earnest Money

If the seller refuses to close and blames you for the incident, you may simply have to sue to get back your earnest money. Most local small claims courts can hear these types of cases, as long as the amount of earnest money involved is small. (Most small claims courts will only hear cases involving controversies of less than $2,000 to $3,000). If the earnest money is more (shame on you for giving so much!), you will need to proceed in the next highest court that usually conducts somewhat informal trials, similar to small claims court. You may need a lawyer to assist you with the court procedure.

SELLER'S REMEDIES FOR BUYER'S BREACH

As you can see, the seller, who has title, is in a better position than the buyer. The seller has three legal remedies for the buyer's breach of contract:

1. Keep the buyer's earnest money
2. Sue for damages
3. Sue for specific performance

Keep the Buyer's Earnest Money

The seller's best remedy is the ability to keep the buyer's earnest money. If the contract calls for the seller to keep the earnest money as liquidated damages, then the seller can keep it, even after selling the property to someone else for full price. In most cases, the buyer will walk away and cut any losses, especially if the earnest money is not significant. If the buyer objects and the money is held in escrow, then the seller and/or buyer will have to go to court to battle it out.

Even if the buyer is in breach, he or she may be able to argue that it is unjust for the seller to keep the earnest money. This argument is not usually successful, unless the amount of money is large and the buyer's breach was insignificant (e.g., the buyer was one day late in obtaining the loan commitment and the seller declared the contract in default). In the case of forfeiting an earnest money deposit, it may be cheaper for both parties to settle out of court.

Sue for Damages

If the contract does not limit the seller's remedy to the retention of the earnest money, the seller can also sue the buyer for actual damages. For example, if the property is in the northeast and the seller took the property off the market for the summer, the seller may now be in a position of having to hold the property through the winter. If the seller can quantify the damages, he or she may be able to sue the buyer for failing to close. Of course, this lawsuit can be expensive, but at least the seller will have leverage if the buyer will not agree to release the earnest money deposit.

Sue for Specific Performance

The seller can also sue for specific performance to force the buyer to purchase the property. This may be futile, for the buyer may not be financially able to purchase the property. It may also be expensive in terms of legal fees and court costs.

DRAFTING THE OFFER

The sample contract provided in Appendix C is fine if you are dealing directly with a seller. It contains all the necessary contingencies you need to protect yourself. If you are making an offer through a real estate agent, however, you must use the standard form. You cannot use your own contract when making an offer through a real estate agent.

The following is a checklist of items to look for when you are buying. Some of these clauses may be found in some form or another in the standard real estate contract that is used in your area.

The Right to Assign

As the buyer, you want to have the right to assign your contract. (See Chapter 2.) In the absence of a statement claiming otherwise, a contract is usually assignable. By placing your name with the words *and/or assigns,* you automatically give yourself that right. However, if the preprinted portion of the contract contains a provision forbidding assignment without the seller's permission, you must cross out that provision.

Inclusions and Exclusions

Most real estate contracts have a clause that specifies what personal property is included in or excluded from the sale. Sellers and buyers often forget to specify certain items, which leads to arguments at closing. A few appliances could be worth $500 or more to you (or cost $500 out of your pocket if you have to replace them). As the buyer, you would prefer the clause, "Anything not specifically excluded will be included, whether or not affixed to the property or structures." As the seller, you would want to include a clause such as "All personal property, including appliances, furnishings, and decorations, is excluded unless specifically included in the purchase agreement."

Disclosing the Third Party

Should you disclose that you intend to assign the contract to a third party? Legally, a purchase agreement is assignable in the absence of any provision that prohibits assignment, as long as the assignment does not unreasonably hinder the seller's rights and obligations under the agreement. For example, if the deal was for $200,000 cash, and the buyer assigned the contract to a third party who purchased the property, the seller is not inconvenienced in any manner. However, on discovering that you made a profit, the seller may be offended or get greedy. We have, on occasion, seen lawyers threaten (unsuccessfully) to sue buyers for misrepresentation after their contracts were assigned for a profit. This effort to bully the investor is silly, of course, because the situation would be no different if the buyer purchased the property for cash, then resold it a day later for a profit. As a practical matter, it may help to diffuse such an argument in advance with an explicit statement in the contract, "Buyer may assign this agreement to a third party for a profit."

Of course, such a clause may also alert a seller into thinking, "Maybe I should ask for more." Whether such a clause is necessary is a tough call, and it depends on the particulars of the deal. For example, if the seller is in foreclosure, divorce, or some other motivation that requires knowingly selling the property below market, it wouldn't hurt to include the clause. But if the reason you got a killer deal is because the seller is ignorant of market conditions (such as an out-of-state seller), you risk blowing a good deal. If you are a licensed real estate agent, the seller may assume you are acting on his or her behalf to get the highest price, so you should disclose that you could get more if you listed the property.

Earnest Money

As the buyer, your preference is for earnest money "to be held in escrow by an escrow agent or a title company of the buyer's choice." Never let the seller hold the escrow. When selling, do just the opposite; keep the earnest money in your account of a title company of your choosing.

Cash Required at the Closing

What happens if you are assuming or taking title subject to an existing loan and it turns out the actual balance of the loan is less than the seller thought? This may mean you have to come up with extra cash at the closing. To prevent such a disaster, insert the clause: "If the actual loan balance is less than as stated herein, the purchase price shall be reduced to reflect the difference; if the actual loan balance is more than as stated herein, then buyer's required cash payment shall be reduced accordingly."

New Loan Contingency

If you intend to obtain a bank loan to purchase the property, you should include a loan contingency in the contract. The loan contingency clause has been interpreted broadly by courts as putting the obligation on the buyer to make reasonable attempts to obtain a loan. Lenders are very aggressive these days, so virtually anyone can get a loan. The issue really becomes how many points and how high of an interest rate you want to pay. The buyer should have a clause that reads similarly to the following:

Buyer is not required to accept a loan with an interest rate of higher than _____ percent over _____ years and payments exceeding _____ /month, and buyer is not required to accept any loan that requires more than $_____ in points, closing, and/or other fees.

Waiver of Escrow Balance

Most lenders escrow taxes and insurance from the borrower each month in an impound account. Typically, the buyer reimburses the seller for the amount in escrow with the lender when assuming the seller's loan. Whether you take title subject to or assume an existing loan, insert the phrase, "Seller agrees to waive tax and insurance escrows held with lender." Using this clause will help you avoid having to come up with a couple hundred dollars in cash at closing to reimburse the seller for an escrow account, the proceeds of which you may not see for several years.

Owner Financing

If the purchase consists of some owner financing, the buyer should look for the following:

- The loan should contain no due-on-sale clause, so the property can be resold to another investor on owner-carry terms.
- The loan should be "nonrecourse," which means that it prevents a judgment against the buyer if the loan is in default. The operative language is: "Seller's sole recourse in case of default shall be against the property, and there shall be no personal recourse against the borrower." Another way to limit your liability is to have a corporate entity, such as an LLC or corporation, sign for the obligation. (See Chapter 12.)

Appraisal Provision

If the contract calls for an appraisal contingency, the buyer prefers one that does not require a licensed appraiser. This will give the buyer an out if he or she can find a local real estate agent who will vouch that the property will not appraise.

Right to Choose the Closing Agent

There's an old saying about marriage that goes something like this: "Choose your spouse carefully, for this one decision can lead to 90 percent of your happiness or misery." For real estate transactions, substitute the words *closing agent* for *spouse*. We cannot tell you how much heartache and aggravation you will save by using a closing agent who understands the double-closing process. As the buyer, insist on the right to choose the title or escrow company so that you remain in control. If the property is listed with an agent, the agent may have a preference of title or escrow company. Offer to pay the full closing fee (usually about $300 to $500) for the right to choose—it is well worth it!

Right to Extend the Closing Date

Most contracts call for a specific date for closing. If the buyer is not ready to close, the seller can hold the buyer in default. Here are some tips for buying time:

- Make the closing date "on or about" rather than "on or before." What does *on or about* mean? This is up to the judge, but we guarantee it will buy you some time. (Of course, when selling, make your closing date "on or before.")
- Have the right to extend the closing date if failure to close is not your fault: "Said date may be extended an additional fifteen (15) days if lender requires additional documentation, paperwork, or actions from the buyer and said delay is not due to the fault of the buyer."
- Have the right to extend for 30 days by paying the seller the equivalent of 1 month's mortgage payment.

Possession

As the buyer, you want possession of the property concurrent with the closing. Typical wording would be, "Possession by buyer to occur upon transfer of deed." If the sellers are living there, make sure you have the right to charge them a hefty daily rent if they are in possession after closing. Because you probably do not want to become a landlord and attempt to collect rent from your seller, it is best to inspect the property immediately preceding the closing and confirm the seller has vacated. If the contract calls for allowing the sellers to remain in possession after closing, consider holding back some of the proceeds to ensure you will get possession when you need it.

Many sellers underestimate the time they need to move, and the longer they are in possession, the more money it costs you.

Also, the contract should state that the property be left "broom clean and free from all debris." A cleaning crew and a hauling truck could cost you several hundred dollars if the seller leaves a lot of unwanted property behind.

How to Draft the Contract When You Sell

Most of the discussion here involves drafting a contract slanted in your favor when buying. When selling a property to another investor, you should use the standard real estate contract that the real estate agents use in your area. This method will make financing easier for the buyer and for banks, and title companies are familiar with the form. Several words of advice:

- Limit the inspection contingency to 48 hours
- Have a short closing date
- Get as much earnest money as possible

A serious investor should have no objection to inspecting the property immediately, putting up $2,000 or more as earnest money, and closing within a few weeks.

Seller's Remedy Limited to Earnest Money

Unless stated otherwise, the seller can keep your earnest money and sue you for breach. Give small earnest money deposits and use the language, "Upon default, seller's sole and only remedy shall be to retain buyer's earnest money." If the seller insists on a larger earnest money deposit, insert a phrase that entitles you to interest at the highest rate permitted by law on your money. That way, the seller will be less likely to hold onto your earnest money for six months while you sue to get it back.

Weasel Clauses

A buyer wants as many contingencies or weasel clauses as possible. If the buyer can get out of a contract without breaching, then the buyer is entitled to the earnest money. The less earnest money you put down, the less you need a weasel clause. If you do need a weasel clause, here are two favorites:

- "This agreement is subject to inspection and approval of the property by the buyer in writing prior to _____."
- "This agreement is subject to attorney approval within seventy-two (72) hours."

Access to Property before Closing

If you intend to flip the property to another investor, you may need access to the property before the closing. If you intend to rehab the property, you have to get access to obtain contractor's bids. Try using the following clause:

Buyer shall be entitled a key and be entitled access to show the property to partners, lenders, inspectors, and/or contractors prior to closing. Buyer may place an appropriate sign on the property prior to closing for prospective tenants and/or assigns.

Create a Standard Addendum

If you are working with real estate agents on a regular basis in your deals, you might want to draft a standard addendum that contains your favorite clauses. You also will have to learn what specific clauses in the "standard" contract used by local real estate agents are favorable and unfavorable to you when buying and selling. Take time to meet with a local attorney to review the standard contract and help you come up with a standard addendum you can use as a template. It is amazing what clauses people (including real estate agents) will accept when part of a so-called "standard addendum." A few bucks spent with a savvy attorney can be a worthwhile investment.

KEY POINTS TO REMEMBER

- Understand the basic principles of contract law

- Put down as little earnest money as possible

- Learn how to draft a contract based on the standard form

7

FINDING MONEY TO BUY THE PROPERTIES

As a property flipper, your ideal transaction would be to assign your contract or close simultaneously with a buyer's purchase, so you have no cash out of pocket. If you have no money and can't find a buyer before your closing date, you would lose your investment (i.e., your earnest money). Furthermore, if you intended to sell the property retail, you would need funds to close, carry, and rehab the property.

Acquiring loans to purchase properties is less difficult than you may think. Many beginning investors are afraid to make offers because they are uncertain how they will get the money needed to purchase. Have faith; if you can negotiate a good enough deal, the money will find you!

GOOD CREDIT IS A PLUS, NOT A NECESSITY

Having good credit will increase your financing choices, but it is not a necessity for buying real estate. You should line up your financing options as soon as possible. This may involve using your own cash, a partner's cash, or a bank loan—or finding another investor to whom you sell the property. As discussed in Chapter 1, always know your where your back door exit is first.

Having fast access to cash means having the ability to close quickly. Often, motivated sellers will accept the lower of two offers because that buyer can close more quickly. Other sellers may accept a lower offer because that buyer's ability to obtain financing looked more solid. As you begin to juggle multiple deals or aspire to purchase properties to hold, your financing knowledge, or lack thereof, can determine how successful you ultimately will be.

USING YOUR OWN CASH

If you are in a market where junker houses sell for $50,000, you can certainly use all cash to buy properties. In New York City or the San Francisco Bay area, however, where junker properties often sell for more than $300,000, this may be more difficult. Furthermore, using cash may not be an effective use of your money, because your ability to make deals will be limited to the amount of cash you have on hand. The sale of a house could be delayed for any number of reasons, resulting in lost opportunities. Rehab properties tend to take longer than originally expected and often go over budget. You should not use all cash unless you have an unlimited supply or have a guaranteed out within a short time. Even if you have a lot of cash, resist the temptation to use it. Experienced investors often reveal that they make some of their worst decisions when they have a lot of cash on hand. In contrast, having little cash forces you to think creatively.

No matter how much cash you have, pretend you don't have it!

Exception to the All-Cash Rule

One minor exception to the all-cash rule is to use your IRA/ SEP money to fund your purchases. You can use this money to buy and sell real estate tax-free. If you do not have a self-directed IRA or SEP, contact Equity Trust Company (http://www.trustetc .com) or Entrust Administration, Inc. (http://www.Entrustadmin .com). These custodians will allow you to use your IRA to buy and sell real estate, make real estate loans, and do other creative deals that most IRA custodians will not allow. Your IRA can even be the buyer and seller of the property, earning the profits tax-free.

Use Your Cash to Bring in Business

As with any start-up business, your cash is best spent in the areas of marketing and advertising. Use your available cash to get the phone ringing with motivated sellers. You may lose a few deals for lack of cash for buying properties, but you will have more overall business. You don't need to worry about disappointed customers, because there are rarely repeat sales in this business.

USING OTHER PEOPLE'S MONEY

An unlimited supply of private money is available for profitable deals. Of course, when you go outside of your own cash reserves for money, you must give up some of the profit. If you do not have enough cash, three options are available:

1. Borrow the money

2. Bring in partners
3. Have the seller finance the transaction

Let's discuss these three options.

BORROWING MONEY

Your financing needs will vary depending on the type of property you select and on how long you intend to keep the property. The focus of this book is on flipping properties, so we won't spend time on borrowing money the old-fashioned way. Whenever you borrow money, you increase your risk of loss, so get your feet wet by flipping a few deals before thinking about borrowing money.

Institutional Financing

If you have spotless credit and a substantial salary or other source of income, borrowing money from institutional lenders is easy. You can easily obtain low-interest loans for investment properties with a 20 percent down payment or more. Some loan programs will permit you to put as little as 10 percent down or even 5 percent down, but these programs are stringent, have high closing costs, and generally require good credit.

If you intend to sell the property to a retail buyer within a few months, you should not be concerned about the interest rate but rather about the cost of the loan. Lenders charge points, which is a fancy name for profit. Each point is a percent of the loan; for example, on a $100,000 loan, 1.5 points amount to $1,500. This fee is paid when you originate the loan. Beware of other hidden charges, such as origination fees, loan review, underwriting, and other garbage fees. They all mean cash out of your pocket at closing. Also, make sure your loan does not have a prepayment penalty, another fee that must be paid when you pay off the loan early.

Once you are more experienced at estimating repair costs, fixing properties, and marketing them for resale, then consider using institutional lending. It is a reliable way to purchase properties.

Friends and Relatives

Sure, friends and relatives are obvious choices for borrowing money, but they may be as skeptical as an institutional lender if you have no experience in real estate. They may also try to boss you around and nag you about repaying the money you borrowed. Do yourself a favor and wait until you have more experience before approaching friends and relatives. Once they see that you're making money, they will come to you.

Private Money

Look in the "Real Estate Classified" section of your local newspaper under "Money to Loan." You will find dozens of advertisements for private moneylenders. The rates they charge are almost criminal—as much as 18 percent with 10 points in fees! While these rates may seem absurd, keep in mind that the availability of the money counts more than the cost of borrowing it. It can actually be cheaper to borrow "hard money" than to use a partner and give up half of the profits.

Many of these lenders (called hard money lenders) will lend without proof of income or a credit report. Their loan criteria are based on the value of the property. They will usually lend anywhere from 50 percent to 70 percent of the appraised value of the property. If you have negotiated a price that is 80 percent of the market value of the property, you don't need to come up with a lot of cash. Institutional lenders, on the other hand, penalize you for negotiating a good deal by basing the loan on the appraised value or the purchase price, whichever is less.

Example: Using a Hard Money Lender versus an Institutional Lender

Let's take a property with a market value (after repairs) of $100,000. This property will appraise for $90,000 in its present condition. You negotiate a purchase price of $70,000. A hard money lender may lend you 70 percent of its appraised value, which is $63,000.

$$70\% \times \$90,000 = \$63,000$$

This means you need only $7,000 of your own cash to close (plus, of course, closing costs). An institutional lender will lend you up to 90 percent of the purchase price.

$$90\% \times \$70,000 = \$63,000$$

Going this route also means you borrow $63,000 and must come up with $7,000. The difference is in the interest rate, which is lower for the institutional loan, but an institutional loan is much harder to qualify for.

Credit Cards and Credit Lines

You may already have more available credit than you realize. Credit cards and other existing revolving debt accounts can be quite useful in real estate investing. Most major credit cards allow you to take cash advances or write checks to borrow on the account. The transaction fees and interest rates are fairly high, but you can access this money on 24 hours' notice. Also, you won't have to pay the loan costs normally associated with a real estate transaction, such as title insurance, appraisals, pest inspections, surveys, and so on. Often, you will be better off paying 18 percent interest or more on a credit line for six months than paying 9 percent interest on an institutional loan, which has upfront costs that would take you years to recoup.

Promotional interest rates are often available on your credit cards, but again, beware. These rates often skyrocket after several months. Chances are, if you have a good credit history, you will be able to raise your credit limits on your existing cards. Creditors do not need to know you will be using your credit cards for the business of investing. Ironically, these creditors would rather see you using credit line increases for typical consumer purchases that depreciate in value and produce no income.

High interest debt must be approached cautiously, and your personality type may not embrace the idea of tens of thousands of dollars in revolving debt. However, avoiding mortgages saves you time and often money, so keep credit cards in mind. You can also benefit by using department store cards with no cash advance features. These cards are available through all the major lumberyards, hardware store chains, and home improvement stores. They will allow you to finance your materials costs, which can add up to thousands of dollars. The interest you pay for the use of this money is tax deductible, so be careful to separate your business from your personal credit card use.

Using a Home Equity Line of Credit

A home equity line of credit (HELOC) can be an excellent financing tool when used properly. A HELOC is basically a credit card secured by a mortgage or deed of trust on your property. You only pay interest on the amounts you borrow on the HELOC. If you don't use the line of credit, you don't have any monthly payments to make. You can access the HELOC by writing checks provided by the lender. In most cases, it will be a second lien on your property.

The HELOC only should be used as a temporary financing source, which can be repaid when you refinance or sell the property. Do not use your HELOC as a down payment or any other long-term financing source—it will generally get you into financial trouble. If you don't pay the HELOC, you can lose your home!

Some institutional lenders won't lend you the balance if you borrowed the funds for the down payment. However, smaller commercial banks that offer "portfolio" loans have more flexibility and may allow you to use HELOC money as a down payment. Once again, use caution when borrowing money in this manner; only do it if the deal is a steal and you can pay off the HELOC money within a few months.

There are limits on the deductions you can take on your personal tax return for interest paid on your HELOC. Generally speaking, you can only deduct that portion of interest on debt that does not exceed the value of your home and is less than $100,000. But if you do your real estate investments as a corporate entity, you can always lend the money to that entity and have the entity take the deduction as a business interest expense. This transaction must, of course, be reported on your personal return, and it must be an "arm's-length" transaction (i.e., documented in writing and within the realm of a normal business transaction). Consult with your tax advisor before proceeding with this strategy.

BRINGING IN PARTNERS

Bringing in partners is a good way to start if you are flat broke and lack experience. But choose your partners carefully. Don't select a partner who contributes the same thing you do—enthusiasm (but no money). Don't pick a partner because that person is your friend or you think it would be fun to be in business together. Instead, choose one who has money and experience in real estate and who can fund a deal that you have negotiated. If you are really green, consider flipping the property to your partner for a quick buck. If you want to see the process through to the retail buyer, and want to make more profit, then using a partner with money and experience can be a worthwhile venture.

How to Split Profits

Every deal will be different, but start the negotiating with a 50-50 profit split. The partner putting up the money and doing the work, such as supervising contractors, may insist on more of the profit. Based on the estimated sales price, purchase costs, and repair costs, you can make a reasonable estimate of the total net profit. If your projected percentage is not sufficient, consider flipping the property to the investor and moving on to another deal.

Joint Venture Agreement

If you choose to take on a partner, you've created a joint venture, which is a limited-purpose partnership. Develop a written joint agreement with your partner that spells out, among other things, the duties of each party and the manner in which money is contributed. (See the sample Joint Venture Agreement in Appendix C.) For a long-term partnership arrangement, consider forming a corporation or limited liability company. (See Chapter 12.)

HAVE THE SELLER FINANCE THE PURCHASE

Having the seller finance the sale, even in part, is the best way to purchase a property. This approach does not require bank qualification, credit, personal liability, or garbage fees. Realize that, if you don't have loan costs involved in the transaction, you can afford to pay the seller a higher price.

Owner-Carry Sale

As discussed in Chapter 2, an owner-carry transaction or installment sale occurs whenever the seller takes less than all cash for the purchase price. Keep in mind that all cash does not necessarily mean you paid cash out of your pocket; it can also mean borrowed money. The less of the purchase price you have to pay, the better the deal becomes—even if you flip the property to another investor. The ideal scenario would be if the seller owned the property free and clear, then took a small cash down payment and a note for the balance of the purchase price. In the real world, however, this rarely happens.

Buying "Subject to" the Existing Loan

As discussed in Chapter 2, when you transfer title to a property without paying off or assuming the existing loan, you are taking the property subject to the existing loan. In most cases, the mortgage or deed of trust securing the existing loan contains a due-on-sale restriction, allowing the lender to call the balance owed immediately due and payable. Some misinformed real estate "professionals" will tell you that transferring ownership of a property without notifying the lender is illegal. At the time of this writing, no such federal law exists, although the state of North

Carolina was considering mandating such a disclosure. Remember that the lender has the *option* to call the loan due but won't necessarily do so. Because you will have title only for a short period of time, this issue is (at least to you) wholly irrelevant. You will have sold the property long before the lender discovers the transfer and decides to initiate foreclosure proceedings. However, check your state law to make sure it does not require written disclosure to the seller or to the seller's lender.

When taking "subject to," be sure that you:

- get a power of attorney so you can deal with the seller's lender for payoff information, or in case you did something wrong with the execution of the original deed and cannot get in touch with the seller;
- get the seller's payment booklet or last monthly statement and send in a change-of-address form, so the statements get mailed to you; and
- have the seller sign a "CYA" acknowledgment about the fact that you are not assuming the loan, which will remain on the seller's credit report until you pay it off. (See Appendix C.)

If you can buy a property subject to the existing loan, you will save thousands of dollars in loan origination costs, closing costs, and other garbage fees. Ideally, you could find out what the seller wants to net in cash from the transactions, then pay the seller that cash and have him or her deed you the property subject to the existing loan. Of course, the total purchase price would have to be low enough for you to make a profit. If the property is in foreclosure, it won't be difficult to convince the seller to deed you the property in exchange for cash and your promise to make up the back payments on the loan and continue making payments.

The problem, however, is convincing a seller who is current on loan payments that you will make payments after the seller deeds the property to you. Remember that, once the seller deeds you the property, the seller has no recourse if you fail to make the payments on that loan. His or her credit will be adversely affected if you fail to make timely payments. So your issue becomes: "How do you convince the seller to deed you the property?" The issue for the seller is: "How do I know you'll make the payments?" The seller wants finality—to have the loan paid off completely and removed from his or her credit report.

You could start by simply telling the seller your intentions— that you will fix up the property and sell it to a retail buyer, at which time you will pay off the seller's loan. In the meantime, you will continue making payments. If your word is not good enough, simply insert a clause into the purchase contract that states:

> Purchaser agrees to satisfy seller's loan with _____
> bank loan #_____ on or before _____ , 200__ , and
> further agrees to make timely monthly payments required by
> said lender, including tax and insurance escrows as they be-
> come due. This clause shall survive closing of the title.

The payoff date should be at least six months out, preferably one year. Of course, the seller's legal recourse is to sue if you don't perform, given that the seller has no recourse against the property. If the seller is savvy enough (or concerned enough) to understand the legal position, offer a second mortgage on the property. This mortgage is for a nominal amount, such as $10, but states that your failure to make payment on the seller's underlying mortgage places you in default of the second mortgage. Thus, if you failed to make payments, the seller would have the right to foreclose against the property to get the title back.

Another way to make the seller feel more secure would be to set up a third-party escrow with a collection company. This company would collect payments from you each month, send them to the lender, and send a copy to the seller. A more practical way to accomplish the same task would be to set up a bank account with a direct deposit to the lender. The bank would send the seller duplicate copies of the bank statements each month. Many banks also have online automated banking services, which require only the borrower's loan number and Social Security number. Either you or the former owner can log in and make or verify payments online.

Installment Land Contract

If the seller won't hand over the deed to the property, consider using an installment land contract. This creates a wraparound transaction in which you make payments to the seller, then the seller makes them to the bank. (See Figure 7.1.) This is similar to the way banks handle car loans; they hold title as security for payment until the loan is paid off. For tax purposes, an installment land contract is a sale, but it puts the buyer in a weaker legal position. If the seller refuses to convey title when you tender the balance of the purchase price, you must sue the seller in court.

Investors don't make money in court; lawyers do. Make sure you approach a land contract with caution and have an experienced attorney review the documents. Also, consider taking a home study course such as "Alternative Real Estate Financing," which provides all the forms and instructions on how to handle installment land contracts the right way. Call Legalwiz Publications at 800-655-3632 or visit http://www.legalwiz.com.

KEY POINTS TO REMEMBER

- Line up your financing before making an offer
- Be careful about using partners
- Learn how to take "subject to" existing loans

FIGURE 7.1 *Installment Land Contract*

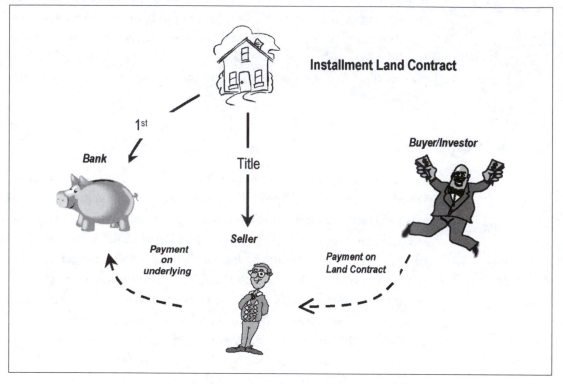

8

THE CLOSING PROCESS

A closing is nothing more than a delivery of cash by the buyer plus an execution and delivery of the deed from the seller. However, many significant events occur between contract and closing. Usually, the real estate agents, attorneys, and title company representatives handle most of these tasks. Whether you do your own closing or use a title or escrow company, become familiar with these tasks.

THE PROPERTY INSPECTION

If the contract calls for an inspection by the buyer, this should happen immediately, especially if a deadline is impending. If the buyer is not experienced, he or she should consider employing a contractor or a professional house inspector. For about $250 in most areas, a house inspection service will prepare a detailed report and provide a list the buyer can use to negotiate a lower price. The buyer can also use the inspection clause to kill a deal that turns out to be a bad choice. If the seller won't agree to make the necessary repairs or adjustments to the price, the buyer can cancel the contract and receive the earnest money back.

If you are planning to flip the property to another investor, be sure to bring interested investors with you when you conduct the inspection. Also, put a provision in the contract that allows you access to the property at reasonable times, so you can easily show it to prospective buyers. (See Chapter 6.)

TITLE AND SEARCHES

A real estate contract usually requires that title to the property be marketable—that is, it must have no serious defects that would prevent it from being mortgaged or sold at a later time. Buyers also want a marketable title, so they can feel secure that no one will sue them or claim an interest in their properties.

A title search is an inspection of the public records that relate to a particular property. While a deed is evidence of ownership, it is not the complete picture; a title is proof of ownership. For example, a deed held by a seller on a land contract is not complete ownership, because the land contract buyer has equitable ownership. (See Chapter 7 for discussion of land contracts.)

The Recording Index

Every county in the United States has a place where records of title are publicly recorded. In most cases, it's the office of the county clerk and recorder or the county courthouse. Records are copied onto computers or microfiche, then recorded in large ledger books. Most areas of the country have begun using computers to index documents.

Understand the Terminology

The giver of any interest in real estate is called the grantor; the receiver of the interest is the grantee. On some documents, the grantor and grantee are called by other terms. For example, on a deed, the grantor is also the seller, the grantee the buyer. On a mortgage, the grantor is also called the mortgagor and borrower, and the lender is the grantee and mortgagee. On a deed of trust, the grantor is sometimes called the trustor, and the lender is the beneficiary.

The most common indexing system is by grantor and grantee. All documents conveying property interests are recorded by the grantor's last name in the grantor index. The same transaction is cross-indexed by the grantee's last name in the grantee index.

Conduct a Title Search

A title search is important because it will determine if a property's title is good and marketable. To determine that, you must follow the chain of title as it changed hands over the years. A break in the chain of title creates a gap, which can result in confusion over ownership. Theoretically, the chain of title must be followed back to the Native Americans, or at least as far as the ascertainable records will show. In practice, the chain of title is only searched back about 50 years.

A title search can be conducted with a title company for a fee. Or, as an educational exercise, you can do it yourself. If you hang around the county recorder's office, you can usually find a title company employee who would be happy to assist you for a few bucks. In addition to the chain of title, make certain you also check for unpaid property taxes, assessments, homeowners' association dues, water and sewer charges, restrictive covenants, court judgments, bankruptcy petitions, and other possible liens that are not recorded in county land records. If this process sounds confusing, don't worry—it is! Be smart and pay for a title search the first few times you buy property. Do not, however, waste time checking title until you have a signed contract with the seller.

Save Money on Title Insurance

Title insurance, like any insurance, defends and pays claims against the insured. In the case of real estate, the buyer is the insured. Thus, if anyone makes a claim against the buyer's interest in the property, the title insurance company must defend that claim and pay any damages suffered by the buyer because of the claim. Consequently, the title company may seek damages against you, the seller. Many sellers have a false sense of security when buying title insurance because they think they are being protected. Holding title in a land trust can help limit your liability on these deals because the title company will not have recourse against you personally. (See Chapter 10.)

Typical claims involve liens not discovered until after the closing, forgeries, errors from previous deeds in the chain of title, and easements or rights-of-way that were not known. While purchasing title insurance may seem reasonable, it can, in some cases, be a waste of money.

If you have little money invested in a transaction, you have very little to lose. For example, if you give a seller $1,000 to deed you the property, what is the limit of your loss? The answer is obviously $1,000, so why would you pay $700 for a title insurance policy if no risk of a title problem was apparent? As you become more experienced, you will see that purchasing a title insurance policy is not always necessary, particularly when you intend to flip the property to another investor for a quick buck. Undoubtedly, that investor will buy title insurance if he or she intends to resell the property after putting up several thousand dollars for repairs.

If the deal is a little thin on profit, simply assign your contract, in which case title insurance won't be necessary.

Let's be clear, however, that we do not recommend you buy and sell property as a beginner without checking title or buying title insurance. This technique must be learned through experience and knowledge. Always do things the conservative and safe way when starting out.

Ask for a Reissue Rate

If you do purchase a title policy when doing a double closing, ask for a discounted rate. If the property was sold or refinanced within the past few years, most title insurance companies will offer a discounted rate, because their risk is lower. Make sure you ask—they won't always offer it up front.

Ask for a "Hold Open" Policy

If you intend to resell the property when you buy, whether in a double closing or within six months, ask for what's usually called a "hold-open" policy. The policy may be called by another name in some states. This type of policy costs an extra 10 to 20 percent up front and will cover title on resale within 12 months. Some companies will cover you up to 24 months. Because the seller usually pays for title insurance, your cost will be 10 to 20 percent of a full policy.

EXISTING MORTGAGES AND LIENS

If you are paying off existing mortgages or other liens, contact the holders of these mortgages or liens for payoff information. Verify that the holder of the lien or mortgage has an original doc-

ument that can be delivered to you when the underlying obligation has been satisfied. Be sure to get original promissory notes
back marked "paid in full." If you are dealing with private mortgage or lien holders, remember to ask for a discount.

Negotiate "Short Sales"

If existing liens are in default, as in the case of mortgage foreclosure, you
can generally build additional profit into your deals by negotiating "short
sales." This process involves appealing to a lender to take its losses early
rather than completing the foreclosure process and spending money on
legal fees. Short sales are not easy to accomplish on first mortgage liens,
particularly in hot real estate markets where lenders know they can resell the property and recoup their money. However, second mortgage
holders are often receptive to discount offers.

To do this, you will have to go through the arduous task of finding
someone at the bank with authority to make a decision. Be patient and
make sure your phone has a speakerphone button, because you may be
put on hold for the better part of a day.

Success Story

A mother of three who works full time, Deborah from Colorado Springs
jumped right into flipping properties after reading the first edition of *Flipping Properties*. She found a seller whose property was in foreclosure, negotiated a short sale with the lender, and flipped it for a $7,117 profit.

THE CLOSING

Generally, title companies perform three services: searching title, selling title insurance, and performing the closing, which is the ceremony of executing and delivering deeds, signing loan documents, collecting and disbursing funds, and recording documents. In some states, attorneys do the title search and the closing. In other states, a separate escrow company performs the closing services. In any case, make certain that the closing agent, attorney, or company is familiar with the double closing process. If you are told it is illegal, unethical, or impossible, contact another service. Double closings are transacted in every state, every day of the week.

The formal closing usually involves sitting at a big oak table at a title or escrow company or in an attorney's office. Both buyer and seller—not necessarily at the same time—sign documents that are held by the closing agent. When the buyer's lender approves the transaction, it funds the loan. The transaction is complete when the funds are distributed and the documents are recorded.

In most states, closings are table funded; that is, the funds are distributed at the table when all the parties finish signing documents. In table-funded cases, both the seller and buyer are present. If you are doing a double closing, you are acting as both buyer and seller. A double closing is really two separate transactions and can be handled in two phases if you don't want your retail investor to meet the seller you purchased the property from. Obviously, you cannot give the seller funds until your investor gives you funds. Thus, one of the two transactions must be closed in escrow until the other is complete. Often, this escrow may last an hour, although sometimes it takes as long as a week. The bottom line is that if your investor does not deliver funds and sign all the closing documents, you can't close with your seller.

Should You Disclose?

Should you disclose in your contract or closing documents that your funds from one closing are coming from the funds of a second closing to a back end buyer? I don't see a problem doing this. In fact, many title and escrow companies are requiring it because of fear of being sued by the seller or the back end buyer's lender, particularly if the back end buyer is a retail buyer and not sophisticated. It doesn't seem logical that a double closing should be a problem, because it's not really any different than closing with cash, then reselling a day later. But with lawyers on the hunt for potential defendants, you can never be too careful.

KEY POINTS TO REMEMBER

- Have the property inspected carefully

- Make sure the title is marketable

- Ask for an appropriate discount for title insurance

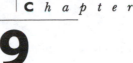
9

REHABS—THE BIG BUCKS

The investor who fixes up a property and sells it to an owner-occupant earns the lion's share of profit on each deal. Because this person must invest the most cash, labor, and time, the retail seller also takes the largest risk. This chapter discusses how to estimate repairs, what items to fix, and how to hire the necessary help to get the job done.

IS THE REHAB BUSINESS FOR YOU?

Before you enter the rehab business, it's wise to decide if this activity is for you. Some people like being hands-on; others are all thumbs and have no business doing fix-up work. Determine whether getting involved in the rehab business is the most effective use of your time. Remember, if you can hire a contractor to handle your projects, you will have more free time to find and negotiate deals.

You may decide to take on a partner who will handle the rehab business while you take care of the financing and the paperwork. Whatever approach you choose, always be involved in managing the process, or it will get away from you. You can't afford to fall behind your schedule or go over budget.

How Much Rehab Knowledge Is Necessary?

Most of your best real estate deals will involve properties that are in desperate need of repairs. Rarely will you find a bargain property in perfect condition. Thus, you need to have a basic idea of how much time and money it will take to bring the property up to salable condition, meaning that it looks clean, new, and attractive. Keep in mind that older houses tend to hold more "secrets." This means your inspector may not discover existing structural problems, subpar repairs, faulty wiring, or other expensive fixes. So keep extra room in the budget for surprises that will show up during the rehab process.

Many real estate investors have become wealthy without having any knowledge of construction. However, an even greater number of investors have lost lots of money because they didn't have enough construction experience. Whether you intend to fix up properties yourself or flip them to other investors, start with a basic rehab job that requires cleanup, carpet, paint, and landscaping. These cosmetic items do not require any special knowledge, just labor and the cost of materials. If you ever tackle bigger projects, such as additions or completely gutting a house, the local building department will usually insist that you also update wiring or mechanical systems. Smaller jobs generally can be done without a permit.

Tip: Do You Need to Get Work Permits?

Ask other contractors about what you can do without a permit before asking the city building department. The city code may require you to get a permit to change a light bulb, but local contractors know what repairs you can get away with without obtaining a permit.

Use the services of an experienced inspection professional to thoroughly evaluate the property before you purchase it. Only buy when you feel comfortable with the level of repairs needed. Just about anyone can remove trash, clean, paint, and landscape a rundown property. Over time, you can tackle more difficult projects. "Sweat equity," or doing it yourself, can earn you extra money on every deal if you have the time available. The more time you spend supervising the project, the more you will learn about the process and the faster it will get done. If you handle a complex project, make sure you have experienced help available and you carefully budget all labor and materials costs.

ESTIMATING REPAIRS

Both beginning and experienced investors habitually underestimate the time and expense needed to complete a renovation. Always estimate repairs conservatively, taking into account the worst-case scenario. Start with the outside and work through the inside, room by room, step by step. Use the checklist in Figure 9.1 to come up with an estimate of repairs, then add at least a 10 percent margin for error. If you sell the property retail, any overestimate will become an extra bonus. If you are a dealer and underestimate the repairs, an experienced retailer will spot this and won't be enthusiastic about doing business with you in the future.

FIGURE 9.1 *Checklist of Repair/Replacement Items*

Checklist of Repair/Replacement Items for an Inexpensive Home	Cost of Materials ($)	Labor Hours	Totals
Kitchen			
❏ Stainless steel sink with faucet	100	3.5	
❏ Ceiling light (use same throughout the house)	20	0.5	
❏ Countertop with backsplash (per 10 feet)	75	2	
❏ Cabinet knobs (for 25)	35	2	
❏ Basic electric range (basic model new)	300	2	
❏ Dishwasher (basic model new/nice model used)	250	3	
Bathrooms			
❏ Vanity with faucet	125	3.5	
❏ Toilet with seat	100	2	
❏ Towel bar set	25	0.5	
❏ Tub surround kit (replaces worn tile)	100	3	
❏ Medicine cabinet	75	1	
❏ Light fixture	25	0.5	
Master Bedroom			
❏ Closet doors (4-foot unpainted)	65	3	
❏ Ceiling fan with light	65	2	
❏ Door (match existing style)	30	2	
❏ Doorknobs (brass set with locks)	15	0.25	
Floor Coverings (professionally installed per square foot)			
❏ Sheet vinyl	2	N/A	
❏ Tile (use 12" × 12" neutral colors)	5	N/A	
❏ Carpet (with pad)	2	N/A	
Other Interior Materials			
❏ Molding (preprimed per linear foot)	0.50	0.1	
❏ Interior eggshell paint (per 5 gallons)	70	8	
Exterior Items			
❏ Exterior flat paint (per 5 gallons)	85	8	
❏ Exterior light fixture (brass)	25	0.5	
❏ Basic single-pane window (installed)	100	N/A	
❏ Window screen	25	0.5	
❏ Front door	150	3	
❏ Roof shingles (installed) 1,200-square-foot ranch	2,100	N/A	
❏ Front porch stoop repair (including labor)	150	N/A	
❏ Seamless gutters (installed per linear foot)	3	N/A	

FIGURE 9.1 *Checklist of Repair/Replacement Items (Continued)*

Checklist of Repair/Replacement Items for an Inexpensive Home	Cost of Materials ($)	Labor Hours	Totals
Landscape Projects			
❑ New sod (installed per square foot)	0.75	N/A	
❑ Juniper bush (3-foot tall)	40	0.5	
❑ 6-foot privacy fence (per linear foot, 8-foot lengths)	10	N/A	
❑ Organic cedar mulch (delivered per cubic yard)	25	0.1	

Can't Even Fix a Toilet!

If you've never so much as picked up a hammer, a repair checklist may not mean much. One way you will become better at estimating costs is to learn how the work is done. That doesn't necessarily mean you learn the physical skills necessary to do each job, but rather you get a grasp of the overall process. Once you understand the mechanics of each part of the job, you will become confident estimating repairs and negotiating with contractors. Major home improvement stores such as Home Depot give free classes on everything from tiling kitchens to replacing windows. Books and videos on basic home improvement are also available from Home Depot, Reader's Digest, and Time-Life. Gathering this information will give you a good idea of the time, materials, and costs of needed repairs. It will also arm you with enough knowledge to know when a contractor is ripping you off.

Learn Costs of Materials and Labor

Spend a few hours in home improvement stores noting the cost of various items you are likely to purchase for your projects. Remember to buy budget-oriented materials. Avoid special order items but look for closeouts or "scratch and dents" when possible.

Once you learn the cost of replacement items, the next step is to determine how much labor will be involved in replacing or installing the items. If you possess basic handy skills, you can do some of the work yourself, following instructions in books and videos. Always assume, however, that you will hire out the labor when calculating repair costs.

In general, basic items cost $0.50 to $1 in labor to install each dollar of material. Thus, a $20 light should cost you $10 to $20 of labor to have it installed. This guideline does not necessarily apply to all items, however. Of course, a $200 light fixture won't cost you $100 to $200 in labor to install. The labor costs will also vary depending on the caliber of labor you employ and the area of the country you live in. Unforeseen problems can also cause costs to rise when replacing certain items.

No exact formula exists for estimating repair costs on a rehab. The truth is, estimating costs is more of an art than a science. Like any art, it takes practice and experience to master. Our goal is to get you thinking and looking for things that may need repair or replacement, so you can come up with a rough estimate. Once you have an estimate, you can prepare an offer to the seller. If you are insecure about your assessment of the property, just reflect that in your offer. Unless the seller is a contractor, you will know more about the cost of doing the repairs than the seller will. Thus, the seller may think it will cost more than necessary to fix up the property and be willing to accept a lower price.

Get Bids from Three Contractors

Whether you intend to do a job yourself or hire help, get three contractors to bid on the work. Spend time with each one and ask a lot of questions. When you hear the same explanation three times, you start to understand it a little better. If one contractor claims a particular project is difficult and expensive, then have the contractor explain the specific issues to you. If another contractor says the job is simple, repeat what the first contractor said and listen to the response. This contractor's answer will help you to determine if someone is fibbing or is more experienced. Be aware that there are usually several ways to address a problem. As you gain experience, you will quickly be able to make sound decisions on how to approach each aspect of renovating a property. Aim for simple, fast, and cost-effective repairs.

WHAT SHOULD YOU FIX?

Many seminars teach investment students a cookie-cutter approach to rehabs. While you should be systematic in your approach to rehabs, please note that every property is different. Location and potential value, age, and the architectural style of a property all affect how to approach the renovation. The condition of the property and the scope of the needed repairs will also affect the rehab process.

How Nice Should the House Be?

Before your fix-up begins, assess the neighborhood, carefully determining the scope of your repairs. You want your house to be consistent with those in the neighborhood—but just a little nicer. You can easily overdo it if you are not careful. Do not go overboard regarding quality of materials, time spent on minor details, or unimportant problems. Only do things that add value and salability to the house.

Beginning investors commonly spend time and money on unnecessary projects. As a result, these beginners must ask premium prices for their properties, wasting time and money waiting for their houses to sell. A rule of thumb is to only tackle projects that will add twice the cost of renovations to the home's value.

Hidden Health Hazards

These days, people are more concerned than ever about their health. Government regulations have increased the cost of rehabbing properties with existing hazards. Once these issues have been discovered and disclosed, you must handle the issue according to the rules. Do the research to see and understand the legislation in your state that affects rehabbing properties. More than ever, it makes sense to go through an extensive inspection process before closing on a property.

Water damage can lead to black mold, a threat to health and an expensive issue to handle. Lead-based paint, used years ago but since been phased out, can be expensive to remove. If you own a property with lead-based paint, make sure you do not sand through the paint, as it is extremely difficult to deal with once disturbed.

Asbestos is another hazard. If it is discovered on ductwork over dirt, the dirt needs to be tested to see if it has been contaminated by pieces flaking off, which usually happens. Some areas require the dirt to be systematically removed by skimming inches off at a time until no asbestos can be detected. Of course, specially licensed contractors are required to resolve each of these hazards.

Radon gas is also common, even in newer properties, and many buyers test for dangerous levels. Mitigation (reduction) is not required, though it may be necessary to take actions that will reduce the levels prior to sale. Lead in water is another concern, so test the water and make sure the water supply line is not made of lead pipe.

While not health hazards, two other expensive and often overlooked problems are faulty sewer lines and termites. If the house is old or has a sewer line that is close to large trees, spend the money to have the line checked by a professional. You can hire a company to use a snake with a video camera to inspect the complete line. Some termites are extremely aggressive and can do tremendous damage to even newer homes. Look carefully for signs of infestation. If you are not experienced in finding them, hire a professional to do an inspection.

Conversely, you never want to have the most expensive house in a neighborhood—just the cleanest. Standard items should be consistent with those in other homes around. For example, window air conditioners may be the norm in one neighborhood, but central air may be standard in another. Don't install central air-conditioning in a window-unit neighborhood. Items such as new windows, sprinkler systems, security alarms, and storm doors are not usually worth the cost and effort to install. On the other hand, do be generous on the cheap items—ceiling fans, doorknobs, switch plates, toilet seats, faucets, trim, bushes, and other cosmetic items.

Locate Help for Repairs

Once you plan the individual projects for a rehab, it's time to decide which projects you will delegate. Balance out your need to learn about construction with your available time. Of course, you will have to pay someone else to complete the projects that are beyond your abilities.

Set Up Network of Helpers

Over time, you will develop a network of helpers. As you get to know other real estate professionals, you will be able to get referrals for most of the contractors you will need. Until then, you can find handy types to fill most of your needs through local newspapers under "Services Offered." You can visit local construction sites to find skilled tradespeople such as roofers, framers, and ceramic tile installers. Often these people are willing to moonlight, saving you money compared with using large companies. Sometimes, though, you will have to refer to the phone book for specialized help.

Paying for Labor

Treat every aspect of a renovation as a challenge to get the maximum value for the money spent. Generally, you can save money on labor by paying cash. There are tax implications regarding cash payments, contractor labor, and employee issues, so consult a tax advisor before you get in over your head. Try to find labor for about $12 an hour, maybe less. You will need skilled contractors for some jobs. Expect to pay these people closer to $25 per hour. Learning a little about each of the various building trades such as plumbing, electrical, heating, framing, and finish carpentry will enable you to critique the work of your subcontractors. Eventually, you will undertake jobs that require the services of licensed tradespeople. Expect to pay a little extra for licensed individuals.

Here are a few tips on hiring:

- Negotiate with contractors, suppliers, and other service providers
- Go with smaller companies to earn discounts and develop loyalty
- Do a reasonable amount of homework on your new associates
- Always be on the lookout for affordable, yet reliable, contractors
- Pay for large jobs on a bid basis
- Ask contractors to show proof of disability and liability insurance

Buying Insurance

Always carry fire and hazard insurance on any properties you purchase. In addition, carry liability insurance once you begin hiring helpers. Most run-down properties qualify for a landlord-type policy, and larger projects can be covered by a builder's risk policy. The builder's risk policy will be more expensive, so use it as a last resort.

Always Get It in Writing

For your large bid projects, you can reduce risk and save money by paying contractors for the complete job. Once you know your contractors and can calculate the time involved in each task, you can pay based on time and materials. Create a written agreement with each contractor you hire. (See sample Independent Contractor Agreement in Appendix C.) Spell out exactly what the contractor is to do, how long it will take, and how you will pay him or her. Do *not* pay contractors in advance; *do* create monetary incentives for staying on schedule. And keep a copy of the contractor's proof of insurance on file.

REPAIRS ON THE INSIDE

Let's walk through the rehab process on a typical two-bedroom, one-bath project house. We will assume the house has working mechanical systems and is structurally sound. We will also assume that you are no Bob Vila but that you can handle basic tasks such as replacing a bathroom vanity and installing a medicine cabinet. If you cannot or choose not to do these things yourself, then factor in the cost of a handy person to help.

Some retailers recommend that you start with the outside of the house to attract potential buyers as early as possible. We disagree.

Never draw undue attention to the fact that you are doing extensive repairs. Working on the inside first will allow you to maintain a relatively low profile. If nosy neighbors or potential buyers stop by, tell them to come back in a couple weeks for a tour. By the time they return, you will have cleaned up the debris, animal odors, and unsafe conditions left by previous inhabitants. Most potential buyers lack the imagination to preview a property in the early stages of renovation. Other than serious investors, it simply does not pay to show the property too early. Once the inside is clean and viewable, start fixing the outside and put up a "For Sale" sign. Or, if you want to earn top dollar, be patient and wait until the project is 100 percent complete before you put up a sign and allow anyone to see inside.

Go with Current Hardware Trends

A recent trend is to use hardware with a satin nickel finish. If you are replacing all the doorknobs throughout the house, this look may be a nice upgrade. You can also select specific bathroom or kitchen fixtures to add the new look. Granite countertops are popular and expensive. You can get a similar look using granite or marble tiles for countertops and backsplash areas. For kitchens, the "commercial look" is in. If you are replacing all the kitchen appliances, you may be able to justify lower-end stainless steel appliances for a designer look.

Kitchen

Because married couples buy most houses, the first place they want to see is the kitchen. The kitchen should be relatively modern, bright, and, like the rest of the house, sparkling clean. Always use semigloss paint in the kitchen as well as in the bathrooms. Wipe cabinets with lemon oil-based products to bring back their shine. If they are dull or dark brown, paint them with a high-gloss white. Use an oil-based primer and replace all knobs and hinges with new ones.

Replace any appliances that are not black, white, or ivory. In fact, if any appliance doesn't look clean and fresh, replace it. You can buy a new stove or dishwasher for a few hundred dollars at a retail chain store, such as Circuit City. For the same price, you can buy a slightly better model at a local secondhand appliance store. Many of the used appliance stores will install the appliance and haul away the old one for a nominal amount.

Unless the fridge is nice and clean, throw it out. Most houses today are sold without a fridge. An ugly fridge looks worse than no fridge, especially if it's large and the kitchen is relatively small.

Putting in a fancy, modern faucet looks great in the kitchen. The best faucets can cost as much as $500, so don't get carried away. You can usually find a quality one on sale for under $75. Make sure sinks and countertops don't date the kitchen, either. Consider replacing the counters with inexpensive units that have a built-in backsplash. You may need an experienced handy person to help you install new counters.

Replace any dated light fixtures with new ones. Chances are you will need professional assistance on electrical projects at first. Take time to learn about electrical systems and always respect their potential dangers. Replace kitchen and bathroom electrical outlets with ground fault circuit interrupter units (GFCIs). These GFCIs help prevent electrical shocks and are required by code in wet areas of new construction, including kitchens, bathrooms, garages, and basements.

In other areas of the house, replace all the switch plates—an improvement that is often overlooked. Most rehabbers paint a unit and leave the old, ugly switch plates. Even worse, some even paint over them. New switch plates cost about 50¢ each, which means you can put new switch plates throughout an entire house for about $20. For the foyer, living room, and other showcase areas, splurge and buy upscale brass plates. They cost about $5 each—not much for the added classy look.

Bathrooms

The bathroom is another important area. You may not be able to enlarge it, but make sure it is modern and bright and that it doesn't smell musty. Use vinegar and lime/rust removal products to clean up porcelain fixtures. If the tub is in poor condition or is not white, have it refinished. Although it will cost several hundred dollars, refinishing a tub is simpler than replacing it. A tile surround in the tub area can usually be repaired and regrouted; however, any plastic ones in poor condition should be replaced. Remove an old shower curtain as well as any outdated window coverings in the house. Replace the toilet and seat if they can't be cleaned to like-new condition. In addition, replace the sink and vanity if they are dated or damaged. Choose a new unit with a one-piece cultured marble top in a standard size.

Paint the bathrooms using a semigloss paint. White is a safe choice, while pale yellow, blue, are green are common in modern houses. A matching wallpaper border along the ceiling can be a nice touch. If the bathroom has old wallpaper that's properly hung and not textured, you can paint over it, using a primer first. But if the paper is textured or peeling, remove it.

Master Bedroom and Other Living Spaces

Ceiling fans are inexpensive upgrades for the bedrooms and living room, unless the house has low ceilings. Always decide where to place fans before painting, and make sure the electrical junction boxes in the ceiling are designed for the weight of a fan. Replace any old or dull light fixtures with new ones.

Check that doors work properly and replace ugly or broken doorknobs. Mirrored sliding closet doors make a room look larger. Verify the height of the existing opening before purchasing them because you cannot shorten mirrored doors. It is especially important that the front door works properly; otherwise you will frustrate potential buyers before they make it inside the property.

Replace any damaged or old brown doors with new white ones. If you are replacing all the doors, consider six-panel, hollowcore doors. They cost just a few bucks more than standard hollowcore doors, but they look very stylish. Doors with a natural or stain finish can be wiped down with lemon oil or a light stain to bring them back to life.

In addition to changing doors, change the knobs. An old doorknob, especially with crusted paint on it, looks drab. For about $10, you can replace it with a new, brass-finished model. Replace bathroom and bedroom door handles with the fancy "S" handles, which cost about $20 per set.

Flooring

Flooring is a major expense in most renovations. Hardwood floors are often hidden under outdated carpets. The hardwood is worth restoring in most cases. Refinishing floors is not a do-it-yourself project. The cost of equipment rentals and the disappointing results that follow provide good reasons not to tackle the project yourself. Professionals will repair, sand, and refinish the floor for as low as $2 per square foot.

Also, look into options for "engineered flooring." These products give the look of traditional hardwood but can be installed by a do-it-yourselfer. We recommend products that are actual prefinished hardwood laminates over manmade surfaces. We also recommend vinyl or tile for flooring for the kitchen, bath, entryway, and laundry room. Tile floors and tub surrounds made good upgrades if you can learn to lay tile or find someone to do it inexpensively.

We advocate installing new carpet throughout the remainder of the house. Carpet can be used in a bathroom to save money if the bathroom floor is in poor condition. Light beige is a safe bet for a carpet color. You can find quality carpeting at bargain warehouses; ask for overruns, which are rolls left over from larger jobs. Many discount carpet stores will discount the price of the carpet if you hire their carpet installers.

Choose at least one grade above the FHA minimum standard and use a closed cell, rebound-type pad. If you can spare the expense, you'll find a berber carpet looks dynamite. Make sure your installers are experienced with berber material; it is not easy to install. Remember, the money you saved by buying a low-end carpet may be lost many times over if the property does not show well.

Mechanical Systems

Make sure every property you sell is in top-notch mechanical condition. Some type of central heating system is mandatory. Quality work shows; even first-time buyers recognize shoddy work. The problems your buyers miss will probably be noticed if they hire a professional home inspector, and these problems may jeopardize the sale. Other well-hidden short cuts could eventually lead to lawsuits, fires, or other tragedies. Fortunately, you will be paid back through personal and financial satisfaction by repairing the property right the first time. It is your responsibility to deliver a safe and sound home.

Carefully evaluate the furnace or other heating system and water heater. If you are uncertain, get a professional opinion or two. It is usually much easier to replace these devices before getting the property in its salable condition.

Adding air-conditioning may be a worthwhile improvement in some areas, depending on the neighborhood. If most homes in the neighborhood have central air, then so should yours. Using window-type air conditioners is worth considering, but don't place these eyesores where they are visible from the street.

Safety Items

Always include battery-powered smoke detectors in each bedroom and in hallways. The National Electric Code calls for hardwired, interconnected smoke detectors with battery backups. However, the difficulty of installation may warrant installation only if other electrical improvements are made. Remember to add ground fault circuit interrupters (GFCIs) to the kitchen, baths, garage, and laundry room.

Make sure the property has securely locking exterior doors. Deadbolt locks should allow the occupant to open the latch from inside the premises without a key (because of fire liability issues). Buyers expect you to provide window screens, a decent roof, and adequate insulation. In addition, each bedroom needs a closet and a safe egress window. Nonconforming bedrooms may hurt the property's appraisal value, so provide at least two conforming bedrooms if possible.

REPAIRS ON THE OUTSIDE

Any property with curb appeal is much easier to sell than a similar property that lags in exterior aesthetics. The exterior items to look for are the paint, entryway, landscaping, roof, windows, gutters and downspouts, mailbox, and the neighborhood.

Painting

Paint goes a long, long way. We suggest giving the exterior of the home an attractive neutral color and a fresh coat of paint. Light colors tend to make a house look larger. Warm shades of tan or gray are easier to keep clean than white. Match colors to the roof and any stone or brickwork. Trim can be painted a separate color to accent architectural highlights, or can be left the same color as the body of the house. Accent the house with basic blues, beiges, and greens. Stay away from wild colors, such as purple, red, pink, and black.

Visit model homes in a new subdivision to get an idea about colors. If the exterior of the house is a nice cedar shingle or vinyl, rent a pressure washer to clean it up rather than paint it.

Entryway

You only get one chance to make a first impression. A cheap front door makes a house look cheap, and an old front door makes a house look old. If the front door is worn or very basic, spend $150 for an attractive new one. Paint it a bold burgundy or hunter green, using a semigloss enamel paint.

Be sure that the entryway is well lit with an attractive porch light. Many older homes have unattractive aluminum storm doors that you should discard or leave in the garage or basement for future owners. Add clearly visible house numbers and a decorative trim around the front door. Remove antennas or other unnecessary items that are visible from the street.

If the front porch has enough cracks to make it unsightly or dangerous, fix it. A wooden porch is fairly easy to repair. Use treated, pressurized lumber and apply stain-and-weather treatment. It does not take specialized skills to fix a stoop; any good handy person could do it in an afternoon. You could have a small concrete porch repaired with a mixable concrete such as Quikrete.

Landscaping

Landscaping should highlight the house without overpowering it. Prune bushes to thin out new growth and cut trees that are too close to the house. In many areas of the country, the front yard should be green and lush. As a last resort, you may have to resod the lawn, but try to salvage it before starting over. Even a weed-infested lawn can look presentable if it is well watered and cut low. Products such as Revive will bring the green back to most lawns but only for a few weeks.

Organic mulch can cover many faults in a yard. Mulch is a natural-looking substitute for grass and flowerbeds. Use it to create beds and borders around the house's foundation and cover weed-infested areas. Use bricks or inexpensive landscape timbers to make interesting beds and borders. Don't use gravel instead of mulch; it costs more and is difficult to work with. Gravel is also harder to remove if a buyer wants to do something different in an area.

If the front yard lacks greenery, plant a few inexpensive shrubs across the front of the house. Old, overgrown shrubs should be removed or trimmed back to a manageable size. Geraniums or other annuals add color during the warm months. When you use your imagination, you will be surprised how much a little effort will improve the outside of a property.

Roofing

The condition of a house's roof is often overlooked by beginning investors and can be expensive to replace. The most common types of shingles are made from asphalt. Check for buckled, cracked, or worn shingles. Use a ladder to get on the roof and take a closer look. If the roof looks good from the street, you may get away with replacing only a few shingles, which is fairly easy but can be dangerous if the roof is steep.

Check to see how many layers of shingles have been applied to the roof. In most areas of the country, two or three layers of shingle are the maximum acceptable. If the roof has three layers or more and looks bad, scrape off one or more layers and apply a new one. This job should be left to the professionals, but shop around for a good price. Keep in mind that when the property is sold retail, the roof may have to conform with higher standards if the buyer applies for an FHA or a VA loan.

A basic 1,200-square-foot ranch house costs about $1,800 to reshingle. If the wood sheathing underneath is rotted, you will need to scrape off all of the layers of shingles and replace the underlayment, which could cost thousands more. Remember that a wood shake roof is much more expensive to replace than an asphalt shingle roof.

Windows

Sandpaper and soap can be used on old windows to get them working again. Window replacement, especially on older houses, is not a job for the beginning rehabber. New windows must be properly installed using flashing to prevent leaks that could lead to expensive water damage. Hire a professional to replace any broken windowpanes and screens.

If you have ugly, aluminum-framed windows, consider adding wooden shutters on the outside. They come preprimed at most hardware retailers and are easy to install. Paint them an offset color from the outside of the house. If the house is dark, for example, paint the shutters white. If the house is light, paint them green, blue, or another contrasting color.

Gutters and Downspouts

A missing section of gutter or downspout can be purchased at a hardware store and installed rather quickly. If all the gutters are bad, consider hiring a professional to install seamless gutters (about $3 per linear foot installed); they look much better than sectioned gutters. If it appears that the house hasn't had gutters in years but has no drainage problem, don't bother installing gutters.

Mailbox

In many neighborhoods, everyone on the block tends to have the same black mailbox. Stand out. Be bold! Spend about $30 for a unique mailbox. For another $50, you can buy a nice wooden post for it. People notice and appreciate these things.

You're Improving the Neighborhood

Sometimes when you improve a property's curb appeal, you also improve the neighborhood. If you are renovating a house that has been in disrepair for some time, you will instantly make friends with the neighbors. Everyone likes it when the "ugly duckling" on the block gets fixed.

On the other hand, an ugly house next door to your shiny jewel will frighten away potential buyers. If the house next door looks like a junkyard, then offer to clean it up. Explain that you will be hauling trash anyway and would be glad to take a little extra. Be diplomatic in your approach when approaching neighbors, for they may be offended or even become belligerent. You can also repair fences, do landscaping, or paint exteriors for adjacent property owners at a reduced cost.

PLANNING THE RENOVATION PROCESS

A vacant house will not make you any money, so don't underestimate the importance of completing the renovation quickly. Plan for the renovation process before closing day. Schedule material deliveries so you can begin work immediately after the purchase. Be prepared to cancel or postpone deliveries and subcontractors if the property does not close on time. Be sure the electric power, gas, and water will be working. It is important to maintain flexibility, which is another reason to minimize the use of special-order items for the property.

Locate Shutoffs

Locate the main electric panel as well as the gas and water shutoffs before starting work. Also locate the city water shutoff near the street. You may be frantically trying to stop the water flow from a broken pipe in an emergency when the water valve in the house breaks. You certainly don't want to flood the house, so shut off the water first.

Rubbish Removal

Plan to remove trash, unwanted carpets, and plumbing fixtures and start any other demolition on the first work day. Be careful of hidden wiring and gas pipes, and don't tear out walls or other potentially structural items unless you are experienced in demolition techniques. In many circumstances, overzealous people have removed load-bearing walls and compromised a house's structural integrity as a result.

As discussed, maintain a low profile during the renovation. Always schedule a trash-hauling service or rent a roll-off trash container for the beginning of the project. If you think you will have major trash removal later in the project, then place the trash in an inconspicuous place such as in the backyard or an extra bedroom. Neighbors are likely to complain if you create a mess or have potential safety hazards they can see.

Replace broken windows at once, and make sure the house is secure. You do not want vandals or curious children inside the property. Once the house is emptied, you can alleviate most odors by airing it out for a few days and by spreading baking soda over plywood floors.

Painting

After the property is cleaned up, next do the painting. Once you have completed any needed drywall repairs, caulk any areas with gaps or cracked paint between moldings, windows, or corners. In addition to caulk, other useful products include construction adhesives such as Liquid Nails and Durham's Rock Hard Water Putty. Before painting, make sure all windows are operable. Use an oil-based, stain-blocking primer to cover dark walls, greasy stains, or smoke damage.

Paints are available in various sheens, from flat to high gloss. While glossy paint looks nice, it shows flaws in the walls. Flat paint is dull, but it hides flaws. Most paint manufacturers sell satin or eggshell finishes, which are between flat and semigloss. Whatever you do, don't buy the cheapest paint—it will cost you double the labor to apply the extra coats that will be needed. Purchase the major brands offered at the home improvement stores and paint store chains.

In less expensive neighborhoods, you can paint over paneling if it is in decent condition. Caulk the seams and nail holes, prime, then reapply caulk to the areas you missed before painting. Copy what builders are doing in the newly constructed houses: they use light beige for all the wood trim and paint the doors white. If the base trim is worn, cracked, or just plain ugly, replace it with pre-primed trim that costs less than $0.50 per linear foot.

Rent an airless paint sprayer for painting an entire house that does not have carpets. Complete the priming and other prep work, masking areas as needed. You can paint a 1,200-square-foot house in a few hours once the prep work is done. You may even be able to paint the inside and outside of the house on the same day. Eventually, you can buy your own sprayer but plan to spend at least a thousand dollars for a commercial unit. You'll find that the less-expensive consumer units are not as reliable or as fast as the high-quality units.

Exterior Projects

Once you have cleaned up and painted the inside (and completed any other low-profile projects), begin work on the property's exterior. Again, remember that once you start on the outside, you may get potential buyers interested, so don't start on the outside until the inside is cleaned and painted. The inside need not be finished at this point, but it should be presentable.

Replace damaged trim and siding, and repair any other unsightly places on the home's exterior. Use paintable exterior caulk and scrape where necessary to prep the exterior for paint. Brick and stucco cracks and mortar problems can be repaired with the help of a professional. Repair gutters and downspouts, then the roof if needed.

To improve the landscaping, begin watering the lawn immediately after starting a new project, and salvage plants that may have been neglected. As mentioned earlier, keep the yard looking green and tidy.

Finishing Touches

Assuming this is your first project, you're likely almost complete with your renovations. Next, install the sinks, faucets, vanities, countertops, toilets, and other hardware. Paint the trim, doors, and cabinets. When all the messy work is completed, let the carpet and vinyl installers do their jobs. A small table near the main entrance is a good place for brochures and real estate agents' business cards.

THE REHABBER'S TOOLKIT

As you get started rehabbing houses for the first time, review this list of tools that you'll need sooner or later.

Automobile

It's not practical to load up your Geo Metro or new Cadillac with building materials on a daily basis. Serious investors either drive trucks or have employees who do. You don't need to buy a brand-new vehicle right away. However, transporting your materials and equipment will eventually become an issue, so be prepared to have the right vehicle.

Tip: Deduct Your Vehicle as a Business Expense

Under Section 179 of the Internal Revenue Code, you can deduct up to $25,000 of the purchase price of your large pickup truck or SUV. To comply with tax rules, you're required to use it 50 percent or more of the time for your business, and it must exceed 6,000 pounds gross vehicle weight (GVW). You can find the vehicle's GVW on the inside of the door jamb of the driver's side door. Realize that you can take the full deduction in the year you purchase it, even if you financed it. If you've been looking for an excuse to buy that big SUV or Hummer, this is your chance.

And, while you're at it, get some magnetic signs to place on the sides of the vehicle that say "We Buy Houses."

Tools

You will need to invest in quality tools if you plan on doing any work yourself. We prefer to buy rather than rent equipment to save time and money in the long run. But, realizing you cannot buy everything at once, start with the basics and always invest in well-made, name brand tools. Power and hand tools are dangerous in their own right, especially if they are of questionable quality. Budget an extra few hundred dollars into each job to buy the tools you will need along the way. In a few years, you will have the equipment to tackle most projects yourself or to supply your crew with what they need to do the jobs safely and effectively.

Even if you never plan on rehabbing a property, keep a clipboard, tape measure, flashlight, screwdriver, and crowbar in your car for inspecting houses that are boarded or abandoned or have no electricity.

Safety Items

Also, purchase a few safety-related items if you do rehab work. Safety glasses, hearing protection, gloves, and a charcoal canister respirator are important for you and your crew. Be sure to keep a five- or ten-pound dry chemical fire extinguisher at each job site.

In addition, let your crew know you expect the work site to be cleaned daily, and you won't tolerate nails left in scrap lumber or other careless habits. A simple injury to yourself or a worker can cost more than you might think. Taking simple precautions will pay off in the long run.

KEY POINTS TO REMEMBER

- Learn about repairs and labor and know what they cost
- Upgrade the right things to be consistent with the neighborhood
- Be generous on installing basic cosmetic items
- Always take safety precautions

10

PRESENTING YOUR MASTERPIECE

Once you finish the renovation process, you should have a sparkling-clean, "new" property to sell. You have done an excellent job of renovating it. Now it's time for the final steps to offer it for sale. You want to make a strong, positive impression to ensure your property stands out from other listings. It will possibly lack character inside and may seem washed out with all the white paint. Each room may blend together in your buyer's mind. The goal is to present your property to potential buyers in a way that screams, "This is your dream home—buy it!"

The process of applying finishing touches and going that extra mile to make your home stand out has become known as staging. The following overview will shed light on how the staging process works. Use this advice, which has proven to be effective for us, as a starting point in developing your own style.

Take advantage of the clean-slate potential of a vacant house to appeal to the buyer's senses. Real estate agents usually assume vacant houses are owned by desperate sellers. Show buyers and their agents you know what you are doing, so they don't try to beat you up on price. Because your property will show well, buyers realize they need to offer a fair price if they want to buy it. Occupied houses may or may not show well, and buyers feel like they are inconveniencing the sellers when visiting their homes. After all, even a home that is well decorated may clash with a particular buyer's taste.

COMPARE YOUR HOUSE TO NEIGHBORING ONES

Before listing your property and holding what you hope is your first and only open house, drive around the block to look at other homes. Look for positive and negative influences on the sale of your property. Paying attention to neighboring houses is especially important. If any of them has trashcans or a broken car out front, an untidy lawn, or other obvious signs of neglect, it is worth approaching the owner or tenants about making changes. Most people will accept your help cleaning up their properties if you ask nicely. As you go through your block, remove old garage sale posters and other signs, all graffiti, and any garbage. Even sweep the curbs. This effort will show off the block as a nice place to live.

It is also important to evaluate nearby listings. Ideally, do a preview of any new listings you did not see before. You should know your competition; your potential buyers will have seen the other houses on the market.

At this point, it makes sense to review the sold comps and expired listings nearby. There is still time to adjust your asking price based on today's market, which may have changed since you purchased the home—even if it was purchased as recently as a few weeks before. Now return your focus to your own property.

GETTING THE EXTERIOR READY

Walk all the way around the property and make sure no trash-cans, recycle totes, garden hoses, or other eyesores are visible. Because the house looks so much better than when you purchased it, you will see problems you did not previously notice. Don't ignore anything that takes away from your property's like-new appearance. Look for additional ways to create curb appeal like adding flowerpots, hanging baskets, or perhaps a wreath or pine boughs if it is winter. Don't think you have to have a green thumb; quality silk or plastic plants can look as good as real ones, plus you can save them to use at future properties.

Remove window screens, then scrape and clean windows and window sills. Knock down any spider webs. Look for and replace any cracked or fogged windows. (If you do not replace them, the property inspector will point them out to potential buyers later.) You can leave some or all of the screens off, stored onsite, to improve the home's views. Remove any paint overspray, and touch up paint and caulking where needed. Sweep the roof and clean the gutters. While on the roof, look for torn shingles or other things that need attention. Paint, tuckpoint, caulk, or replace any weathered penetrations such as flues, chimneys, or roof vents. Water the lawn, remove weeds, mow, edge, and apply Revive or a similar product if the lawn is not in peak condition. Take off dead blooms, prune shrubs and trees, and add new colored mulch or pine straw to create a fresh appearance. You can use weed-blocking cloth for landscaping, but make sure it is completely hidden by the appropriate ground cover.

Be sure the house is an inviting place to enter by making the walkway to the front door well lit. If the approach to the front door is dark or potentially unsafe, add low-voltage lighting. It does not have to be elaborate or expensive. Just place four to six solar-powered lights along the walkway so visitors can see where they are going. (Because solar-powered lights are removable, you can take them with you for the next property.) Make sure the doorbell ringer is lighted and has a pleasant tone. Many buyers like to ring the doorbell before entering, so do not let them start their tour by finding a broken doorbell. Check all doors to see if they work properly. Buyers will not tolerate squeaks, large gaps, sticking, or difficult-to-use keys. Place new doormats at each entrance. These mats welcome visitors and also help protect carpets and flooring.

Now it is time to prepare the inside of your home.

GETTING THE INTERIOR READY

Builders spend thousands of dollars on interior decorators and expensive furnishings of their model homes because they know what sells properties: emotion. You do not necessarily need to furnish the entire house with new, quality furnishings, but you can add a touch here and there. The idea is to have buyers fall in love with your house; they will want to purchase the house out of emotion, rather than logic and reason.

Start by making sure every inch of the house is as clean as possible. Wipe all woodwork and cabinetry with oil or rejuvenating cleaner. Polish or seal hardwood floors if needed. Remove all dust from vents, ceiling fans, cabinets, and horizontal surfaces. If there is any doubt about the carpets, have them professionally cleaned. If the carpet is new, make sure all loose pieces are vacuumed up. If there is a fireplace, have it cleaned by a chimney sweep. You can even stick in a few logs or have an electric "fire" log going for effect.

If you have not done so already, replace the thermostat with a basic, programmable model. Discard and replace anything that looks "used," such as sink strainers, ice-cube trays, fireplace grates, and range drip pans. Replace only the things that would be noticed as missing. Walk throughout the house at a quiet time to listen for squeaks in doors, creaky floors, or any other sounds that can be eliminated. Make sure every light bulb in the house is working and every toilet paper and paper towel holder is filled.

Entryway

The first impression is the most important. If the entryway or foyer is dull, add accent rugs and a small table. On the table, put a Plexiglas holder with copies of an information flyer about the property and a place for real estate agents to leave their cards.

Decorations

As with paint, decorations should remain relatively neutral, although you can add color and texture. Wall hangings, attractive curtains, and certain paints can be neutral yet add personality to a home. Try to maintain a decorating style that complements the architecture and the age of the home. A warm, yet understated look lends a comfortable feeling to a home.

Displaying vases, potpourri bowls, and candlesticks are just a few ideas. Dried flowers and pinecones, along with other items found in nature, can be placed almost anywhere. Go to thrift stores, garage sales, and discount chains (e.g., Marshalls, Ross Dress for Less) that carry discontinued or slightly damaged items. Start collecting a set of colorful towels, soap dishes, chairs, side tables, fake plants, pictures, and other accent items you can store in your garage or basement.

Furnishings

There is no need to furnish a house with bedroom furniture or other large pieces. For high-end homes, you can rent complete bedroom sets, but sometimes an air mattress on four milk cartons with attractive linens will do the trick. Small or odd-shaped spaces can provide decorating challenges and often leave buyers with a negative impression. If your property has such an area, make an extra effort to furnish it in a way that shows there is a solution. Displaying a dining room table complete with chairs, placemats, and a nice setting creates a homey atmosphere. If the furnishings fit the dining room well, you can even negotiate the sale of the house to include these items.

Floors

In homes with floor coverings other than carpets, use throw rugs throughout. With beautiful hardwood floors, use rugs as accents. You can use larger rugs to hide unattractive floors.

Lighting

If the bedrooms and living room have no overhead lights, add a few floor lamps. Keep key lights on at all times, and ask people going through the house to keep the lights on. In fact, you can make a house look much nicer simply by experimenting with differing varieties of light bulbs in the right places.

Plants

Small plant stands will add appeal and keep plants off the floor. You can purchase standing ficus or palm trees and place them in fancy pots. Dried flowers are easier to deal with and silk flowers are even easier. Craft stores such as Michaels have an unlimited supply of these items.

Kitchen

The kitchen is the heart of the home, so make it look lived in. Place a set of dishtowels, paper towels, and even glass jars with colorful contents on the counters. Show off tinted glass vases or sun catchers in front of windows to add warmth. Make sure the oven, refrigerator, and stove are clean. As discussed earlier, an ugly refrigerator can detract from the kitchen's appeal, so consider replacing it or throwing it out. A message board with little notes on it gives it a nice touch, as do magnets on the fridge with shopping lists and kids' drawings. (Get your own kids to draw them for an authentic look!)

Bathrooms

In the bathrooms, place matching towels, soap, and tissue dispensers and a candle or plug-in air freshener with a pleasant scent. Put attractive shower curtains in the bathroom, but pull them aside to show off attractive tile work. For just a few more dollars, a colored shower curtain and decorative curtain rings look great. A nice floor mat and magazine rack give the bathroom a lived-in feel.

Wall Hangings

Place a few pictures, wall hangings, and a mirror or two throughout the house—one item in each bedroom and at least two in the kitchen and family rooms. Hang the pictures on the walls, at or below eye level, or simply lean them against the walls at floor level.

Window Coverings

Window shades give character to any house. Use them in the front windows and in other rooms that may have especially bad views, including finished basements. Pleated shades block marginal views while letting light into a room, whereas miniblinds provide a cleaner look without hiding what is outside. Home improvement centers carry inexpensive blinds that can be custom-sized while you wait. Blinds with large, two-inch faux wood slats are affordable and especially nice. For basement windows, you can even use the temporary paper shades to camouflage an ugly window well.

The Power of Smell

Do not underestimate the power of smell. Appealing scents can leave a lasting impression on people. You want potential buyers to associate a pleasant fragrance with your property, even if that association is on a subconscious level.

Start by neutralizing any existing unpleasant or musty smells created by mildew, lack of fresh air, or garbage. Even though the house is immaculate, there will be lingering fumes including new paint, carpet, adhesive, or floor sealants. If possible, open all windows during the final few days of preparation, keeping air moving through all parts of the house. If necessary, bring in portable fans to help circulate fresh air. Sprinkle baking soda throughout the house, leave it for several days, then vacuum using a clean bag. Use natural cleaning products such as vinegar and citrus oil in this last stage to avoid a hospital-like smell. Lastly, use natural air fresheners such as fresh-cut flowers, pine boughs, or potpourri. Plug-in air fresheners work well, too, particularly in bathrooms.

Unfinished Areas

Don't forget to inspect the basement or crawlspace, attic, and other unfinished areas and add lighting to them. Even battery-powered lights are better than nothing. Make sure these spaces are completely clean. It's surprising how many listings have construction debris and other unsightly items lying around. If an ugly window well is in view from the basement, clean it out and paint it a neutral color.

It's fairly common to make unpleasant discoveries when you visit these unfinished areas, even when the house appears to be well prepared. You may encounter sewer-line debris, mousetraps, animal remains, furnace filters, ducts full of construction debris, building materials, cigarette butts, and drawers full of sawdust. Your goal is to show every space in the best possible way. The only evidence of renovations should be well-marked cans of paint, spare shingles, and similar items in an appropriate place. It is also worthwhile to have an area to display product warranty information and a sprinkler system map with winterizing instructions. These items would typically be on a table or counter, along with other information regarding the property, loan options, homeowners' association information, and positive information about the neighborhood.

Additional Considerations

Equip each room with a light-sensing nightlight so potential buyers can find their way around. Remember that many showings take place after dark, so the house should seem safe and be easy to view any time of day. If a hallway or other space has no light switch, installing a wall-mounted remote control switch is a simple fix. These little improvements can make the difference between your property's selling or not. We suggest you place small handwritten signs throughout to point out various features. These notes will have the effect of a guided tour as they highlight selling points that may otherwise be unnoticed. For example, you can point out dimmer switches, a special thermostat, appliance features, wiring upgrades, cable or computer outlets, architectural highlights, or anything new.

Assess the property to see where it falls short of current building codes. As a minimum, provide new smoke detectors, grounded receptacles, and ground fault circuit interrupters throughout. Most starter homes are purchased by families with children, so it pays to identify and remove potential hazards. Examples include railings with wide spacing between slats, sharp edges, windows exposed to large drop-offs, easy access to unfinished areas, and dangerous areas outside. You cannot eliminate all hazards, but you can make improvements such as adding latches or locking handsets, sanding sharp edges, and placing strategic buffers such as furniture.

Engage Others to Help with Appearance

Because the idea is to upgrade the appearance of the property, don't use cheap-looking items or those that might appear too personal in taste. Even if you feel qualified to make all the decisions regarding your décor and presentation, it would be wise to get second opinions from interior decorators, friends, or real estate experts. Visit show homes in new neighborhoods to gather ideas and possibly borrow a few items from your own home if you don't feel too much sentimental attachment to them.

Consider hiring professional companies that will decorate and furnish the entire house. Depending on its size and price range, this may make sense. It is not uncommon for sellers to pay more than $10,000 to professionally decorate a $1,000,000 home. We feel this may be overkill in a small starter home or condominium under $250,000. Although the term *stage* is trademarked, it has become a common expression in the industry to refer to the process of decorating a home specifically for resale.

Web sites with excellent information include:

- http://www.simpleappeal.com
- http://www.stagedhomes.com
- http://www.homestagers.com

TAKE AN EXTRA WEEK TO GET IT READY

Because presentation is so important, make sure you leave enough time to do it well. Once the house is empty and you have completed all known projects, expect to take up to ten hours to thoroughly clean it. We advise hiring a professional cleaning company for this step. Then walk through the property; you will be amazed at how many things stand out that still need to be addressed. Invite friends over to get their honest opinions on any improvements to make. Once you have done the "final cleaning" and received second (and third) opinions, you can add the decorations. Then (you guessed it!) clean it more and get additional opinions. Because more and more listings are being presented in such a professional manner, you have to do a better job than your competition. You can take pride in showing the property—and be ready for that quick sale.

Lastly, remember that properties being shown require ongoing cleaning to look presentable. Properties that have been renovated will continue to show residual dust from sanding floors and drywall. Some listings have signs asking people to remove their shoes. While this practice, in essence, points out clean or new carpets, it does not invite potential buyers to "make themselves at home." Builders showcasing immaculate new homes do not ask such things of buyers. We do not recommended doing so, either.

Fortunately, most people respect other people's property, especially when accompanied by their real estate agent. Still, it is amazing how much of a mess inconsiderate people can make when looking at properties. They sometimes track in dirt, leave their trash behind, leave water running, and do not flush toilets after using them. Recently, someone left a window open during a tour of one of our vacant listings. When it got cold later that night, a pipe burst and did major water damage to the bathroom and hardwood floors. In addition to the cost of repairs, several potential buyers were left with a bad impression, so we had to take the property off the market while repairs were completed.

Visit your property often to clean floors, dust, tend to lawns, and check for any problems. By the way, be wary of "walk-up" buyers who want to come in and look around. If you are alone, invite them back for a scheduled appointment with you or their real estate agent. It is not worth risking your safety. And if the house is not yet on the market, get their contact information and invite them to the open house.

KEY POINTS TO REMEMBER

- Compare your house to those in the neighborhood and add finishing touches

- Find ways to add curb appeal inexpensively

- Pay attention to details inside the house and ask for expert help with decorations and furnishings

- Clean the house thoroughly, adding extras to make potential buyers feel welcome

SUCCESS IN A CHANGING MARKET

We get a lot of questions from people asking, "Will your approach work in my market?" Just as often, we hear ignorant statements such as, "This approach won't work in my market," to which we respond, "Then move out, so it will work for someone else!" The truth is, flipping—buy low, sell high—works in every market, but you need to learn your market and adapt the techniques in this book that it requires.

There are many ways to describe real estate markets, including "hot" versus "flat" or "rising" versus "falling" or "buyer's" versus "seller's." Remember, to survive and profit as a flipper, you must buy at an appropriate discount, allowing you to sell the property for a profit. Real estate markets are subject to fluctuations, but these fluctuations typically do not greatly influence the ability for the informed flipper to make a profit. In fact, flipping can be the least risky way for a beginning investor to make a profit in an uncertain market simply because of the relatively short amount of time the flipper will own the property. Unlike the stock and commodities markets, real estate markets don't rise and fall rapidly. For long-term investing, discussed later in this chapter, additional market factors are important to your buying decision. Flippers who plan for short-term real estate market appreciation are speculating, which is outside of the basic model of flipping.

WHAT IS THE IDEAL MARKET FOR FLIPPING?

Let's be clear: there is no such thing as an ideal real estate market for flipping. It tends to be more difficult to find bargains in rising markets, however, because if the market keeps rising, the probability of selling the property quickly for a large profit increases. In contrast, when property values are falling, more so-called bargains become available. Yet you need to assess the true value of these properties based on when you expect to sell the property. Thus, your purchase must be made at a steep discount to allow for a profitable sale later.

Basic Strategies to Use

Some basic strategies can be used successfully in virtually all market conditions. Most of the following discussion is based on selling properties to owner-occupants, although similar rules apply to wholesaling properties to other investors.

Become educated in your local market first by understanding the large-scale trends—from global down to national, regional, and specific neighborhoods. Learn about target neighborhoods, enlisting the aid of successful real estate professionals along the way. These professionals will help interpret market indicators, such as the average length of time houses are sitting on the market this month versus last month or last year. Armed with this type of information, you will be able to make good decisions.

Rising Markets

Many would-be flippers complain about the high-priced, limited-supply markets that typically favor sellers. These conditions have been common in many parts of the country in recent years, providing certain challenges to acquire properties at below-market prices. However, once a property is secured at an attractive price, you have a great chance of success to sell it at a healthy profit. Even if it takes a relatively long time to renovate and sell a property, you have the advantage of being able to ask a higher price in a rising market.

Inventory Trends

Inventory, defined as the number of properties offered for sale, is a good indicator of current market trends. If inventory is low because of building restrictions or geography, then high demand will lead to rising prices. In rising markets, sellers often capitalize on the excitement of new listings to get properties under contract quickly, at premium asking prices.

There are also seasonal fluctuations in inventory, such as fewer listed properties in the winter months than in summer and a surge of listings in the spring. Some areas, such as resort destinations, follow seasonal trends. Generally, seasonal drops in inventory reflect the trend to market properties more aggressively in spring and summer months when real estate markets are more active. Properties sell year-round, though investors should plan to reduce the price for winter listings or at least know that properties take longer to sell during those months.

> ### Speculation on Market Appreciation Can Be Risky
>
> Since we first wrote this book in 2001, some speculators have made a bundle buying up "preconstruction" condominiums in hot markets, then selling them for 25 to 50 percent profit after the project is completed, often only a year later. Properly timed, a preconstruction condo purchase can be lucrative if supply is limited (such as on a beachfront) and the local market is strong.
>
> However, the basic premise of such activity violates our number one rule, which is to make your profit when you buy, not when you sell. If you are paying full price at what could be the top of a saturated market, you may find yourself stuck with an overpriced property or bailing on a large earnest money deposit.
>
> If you do sign a contract to purchase a preconstruction property, make sure the builder does not prohibit you from flipping the property. Also, have a Plan B—if you can't sell it, can you complete the purchase and rent the property to ride out a market cycle? Check the fine print to see what you are committing to and how much money you have to put up before the project is completed. And be mindful that construction projects often get delayed for a variety of reasons, so make sure you are dealing with a reputable builder.

Falling Markets

Often, property values are flat or falling in a particular area. This type of market offers great opportunity to the savvy investor. When property values are falling, inventory often rises, and many sellers become highly motivated when their properties fail to sell quickly. Motivated sellers will do whatever it takes to sell their property. Whether sellers need to move from the area, are struggling financially, or have other pressing reasons to sell, they may well accept a below-market offer. Investors know that a weak market can offer extraordinary deals, though flippers need to proceed with caution. In a falling market, even a few months' delay can turn a sound deal into a headache. It always pays to know the market and purchase the property at a price low enough to net an eventual profit, even if the market continues to fall. The common myth is that you cannot make money by flipping properties in a bad real estate market. In a bad real estate market, you can often buy "junker" properties for 50 cents on the dollar and sell them for 60 cents. It's all in how you do the math.

It is also worth noting that markets can and will change. If the market rebounds after a purchase, then all is well for the investor. However, if the market takes a downturn after a purchase, there can be trouble ahead. Markets commonly show signs of slowing or turning over several months. Sometimes the early signs come from national economic trends, such as rapidly rising interest rates or sweeping changes in tax policies that affect homeownership or investment (e.g., the rapid change in depreciation rules for real estate investors in the late 1980s). More likely, clues come from local market conditions, such as unemployment, oversupply, or a change in demand because of living conditions.

Sellers often choose not to believe the market is changing, making it difficult to convince them to accept a low offer. In these cases, it is best to move on to the next deal, even if it means fewer purchases for a few months. It is also worthwhile to follow up with sellers who weren't highly motivated. Sellers' attitudes and situations can change over several weeks or months of trying unsuccessfully to sell their properties. Eventually, reality may set in and these sellers will be forced to discount their prices.

When it comes time for an investor to market a property in a weak market, it will need to stand out in its price range. The property can still sell quickly, but buyers have a larger selection of homes to choose from, so you need to do several things to assure success. First, your budget must allow for a longer time to sell. Second, the finished product must be better than the other listings being offered, both in appearance and price. Third, the flipper must have a good marketing plan, ideally with multiple exit strategies.

Most likely, the property will sell quickly if it fits this description. However, if it does not sell, then the low purchase price allows room in the budget to carry the property for a longer period of time. Ideally, if it simply did not sell and is not showing signs that it will sell anytime soon, you would have the option of holding the property as a rental. That is a better option then being forced to "give it away." In many cases, if you cannot sell the property in a few months, you can hold it and rent it for several years, then sell it at a profit.

BALANCED MARKETS

Real estate markets are usually closer to being balanced than they are to being at either extreme. In a balanced market, prices are rising at or just above the pace of national inflation. Houses within the median price range for the metropolitan area will sell, on average, within 60 days. While markets are constantly changing due to circumstances beyond anyone's control, an equalizing effect exists in a free market economy. Often, a market will exhibit some tendencies of each of the balanced, falling, or rising classifications. And within a particular market, houses will be selling better or worse in some pockets than in the metropolitan area as a whole.

There is profit to be made in a balanced market, following the buy-low/sell-high premise. Remember, as soon as you have the market figured out, it will change! Experienced investors may have an advantage in seeing trends, but no one can foretell the future, and short turnaround deals usually involve the lowest amount of risk.

EXIT STRATEGIES

More important than guessing the future of a local market, you need to have a clear plan in mind when purchasing property. (This section expands on the lessons from Chapter 4.)

Your strategy may be to take title, then wholesale the property to another investor within a few days, or perhaps rehab and sell it within a few months. Typically, flippers are in and out quickly, but the entire process of purchasing and reselling a house can take a varying amount of time. If you're flipping it, you may want to hold the property long term. Usually the quickest turnaround comes from selling to another investor. Often, an investor will simply assign the purchase contract, netting the flipper a healthy profit with a minimum investment and an extremely short turnaround time.

The Quasi-Rehab

In hot markets, you can flip properties directly to the retail market with little or no rehab work. If the property is in relatively good shape, it may only take decorating to get it ready for resale. Even if the house needs a moderate amount of work, you can take the rough edges off the project and offer it as a minor fixer-upper. A good cleanup and painting often do the trick. Usually that process takes just a few days; then you are ready to offer the property for sale.

As an investor, your choice of financing should be based on the expected time from loan initiation to loan payoff. It can make sense to use a credit line with a high interest rate and low closing costs if you plan to flip the property in a few days or weeks. However, tying up readily available funds for months can create an opportunity cost of turning down other deals, plus interest costs can get quite expensive. If possible, try either to buy the property subject to existing financing or simply tie up the property with a pur-chase contract that gives you the right to enter the house and start doing rehab work.

Offering Terms

Attractive financing terms have been used to move products in a variety of markets—from cars to furniture to computers. Like-wise, you can move difficult-to-sell properties by offering attrac-tive owner-financing terms. Having alternative financing available attracts buyers with limited choices. These terms may include helping with the down payment or financing some of the pur-chase price with a seller carryback note and mortgage. Making prearrangements to help buyers with financing can prove quite valuable in selling your properties. In addition, sellers who offer attractive terms can get a higher price than sellers who ask for all cash to buy a comparable house.

Don't Raise the Price Beyond the Legitimate Appraisal Price

While it is possible to get a higher price for a property when offering terms, you cannot raise the price beyond its legitimate appraisal price. As discussed earlier, you may run into unethical dealings, including false representations of property values, loan fraud, and other questionable practices sometimes associated with flipping. We do not support those practices and recommend seeking representation by legal counsel re-garding the way loans are structured.

Look for advantages of flipping not only for cash but for terms. In other words, instead of buying and flipping for all-cash profit, you accept a note for some or all of your profit.

The going rate for an owner-financed note is generally much higher than what big lenders offer and certainly more than you could earn in a CD or money market account. For example, if the going rate for a mortgage is 7 percent, you could get 9 percent or higher. And you can sell the note for cash at a later time, so you still have liquidity in your investment.

The bonus of taking "paper" (an owner-financed note) for your equity is that you can demand a higher price. Cash always buys a discount, so if you can offer a buyer a way to get into the property with less money down, you can raise the price.

The risk of taking back a note, of course, is that the payor could default. The note will generally be secured by a lien (mortgage or deed of trust) on the property, but this lien will be junior to another lien, so you risk losing your position if the senior lien is in default. When you sell, make sure you have all your cash out of the deal, so you are not reaching into your pocket if the borrower defaults.

Lease/Option: Best of Both Worlds?

Another variation may be to refinance the property after you have rehabbed it, getting all your money out. Then, you could sell the property on a lease with an option to buy. If your tenant exercises the option after one year, you will fare better on taxes then if you had sold it quickly. You can do a 1031 tax-deferred exchange, which allows you to roll your gain into another property purchase and defer paying taxes, or just pay the capital gains rate rather than the ordinary income rate. In the meantime, you may be able to enjoy positive cash flow. You can find more information about lease/options at http://www.legalwiz.com.

Keep in mind that, if the tenant does not exercise the option to purchase, you are stuck with the property. If you are at or near the top of your real estate market cycle, you may end up with a property you cannot sell right away, becoming a long-term landlord.

Rent It

While acquiring rental properties is not the foremost goal of most flippers, the subject deserves some attention. Many mainstream properties targeted by flippers (starter homes) can make excellent rental properties. If you have money tied up in the deal, you can refinance it to recoup most of your capital and lower your monthly payment. The option of holding onto a property that fails to sell in the desired time frame can be a good Plan B. Then, you can place the property on the market at a later date or hold it indefinitely. There are sound reasons to consider building wealth through equity as part of a flipper's long-term plan. Armed with the knowledge of multiple exit strategies, you can increase your opportunities for success.

THE GREAT DEBATE: FLIPPING VERSUS HOLDING

This book focuses on flipping—that is, turning over properties quickly rather than keeping them long-term. In some cases, holding property will generate more long-term wealth for you than flipping. Therefore, you may consider flipping some properties and holding others. Or you may consider flipping for a while, then begin holding properties later. The big question is, "When should you hold versus flip?"

The Advantages of Flipping

The main advantage of flipping is that you get your cash out now rather than later. For many people, the certainty of getting a paycheck right away is highly appealing. Flipping takes the real estate market out of the equation; if you buy a property correctly, the market is almost irrelevant except concerning how long it will take to resell the property. Of course, if you buy cheap in a soft market, you can afford to hold a property six months instead of two.

Flipping is generally good for your cash flow, which is important in any business. However, if you purchase houses and acquire too much equity and not enough cash, you may get into a cash crunch if you don't have additional income.

Don't forget that you can flip houses as a part-time or full-time business. You can do as much or as little as you want and can take a break from your flipping business when you desire. In short, once you empty your inventory, you are not tied to your business. You can take long vacations or pick up and move to another city and start over.

The Disadvantages of Flipping

The main disadvantage of flipping is that it is "hands-on" income. Once you stop flipping, you stop making money. If you are young and like to work for a few months, then take a few months off, that's fine. But at some point, you will realize that, if you keep spending the profits, you don't accumulate wealth.

Also, if you flip, you lose the benefit of market appreciation. While gauging the market is a risky venture, a good market timer can gain wealth quickly with little effort by buying properties at the right time in emerging markets. In the last five years, we have seen many investors get rich simply by being at the right place at the right time. On the other hand, if you buy a property in the wrong place at the wrong time, particularly for the wrong price, you can end up with a property you cannot get rid of quickly enough. You could also get in over your head in a rehab project and have to bail, losing tens of thousand of dollars.

As discussed in Chapter 13, you cannot take advantage of certain favorable tax laws on flipper properties. One particular loophole not available to the flipper is the 1031 tax-deferred exchange. Also, flipping can have a negative consequence if your real estate activity is more of an investment and you don't want taxable income. If you flip, you have a gain; there's not a lot you can do to hide that income.

Finally, if you don't spend all of your income on living expenses, what will you do with it? A diversified portfolio is a good idea—you could put some of this cash in bonds, money market, mutual funds, and so on, but you might earn a better return by leaving your profits in real estate rather than taking them out.

The Advantages of Holding

Property holders can generate true wealth over the long term. Historically, property values in the United States have appreciated at a rate greater than inflation. If you buy in the right neighborhoods, your annual appreciation may reach double digits. You can use properties with equity as collateral. You can provide rental income for your retirement years, and you can pass property down to the next generation. Once your properties are owned free and clear, you have passive income that pays you even when you are not working.

The Disadvantages of Holding

The main disadvantage to holding is that your assets are not liquid. Unlike stocks or bonds, real estate is not easily converted to cash. When selling real estate, you have to locate a buyer, then pay closing costs, title insurance, real estate commissions, and possibly a local property transfer tax.

If you must sell when the market is down, you will not get the best price. If you have a tenant in your property under a lease, you cannot simply kick the tenant out. You have to wait until the lease expires, pay the tenant to leave early, or hope to find a buyer who doesn't mind having someone living in the property. And, of course, the future is always uncertain. While real estate may have appreciated in a particular area an average of 10 percent over the last 20 years, it may not do so in the future.

If you hold properties, you also risk running into negative cash flow. There may be times when your properties are vacant or need repairs, and you have to dip into savings to feed the proverbial "alligator."

WHAT'S RIGHT FOR YOU?

The more important question is not whether flipping is better or worse than holding but rather whether flipping is right for you. Ask these questions:

- Do I need additional income now or in the future?
- Am I in a high income tax bracket and so would be adversely affected by earning more income now?
- Does my local real estate market present opportunities to acquire bargains, yet does it still command high rents that would cover my expenses if I needed to hold onto the property?

- Do I have other income or savings that I could tap into in case my rental properties become vacant or need repairs?
- Do I have the time and patience to deal with tenants?
- Is the local real estate market rising or falling at this time?

Most investors start out flipping houses, then gradually work into managing rental houses or becoming involved in larger, more complex real estate projects. Some people don't have the temperament to deal with tenants and the headaches that come with rental properties. Some look for side income by flipping. Others want to quit their jobs and make flipping houses their full-time business.

Consider all options, including a mixture of flipping and holding properties. Be sure to reevaluate your financial goals on a regular basis and adjust your real estate strategies to support your goals.

KEY POINTS TO REMEMBER

- Learn to identify your market
- Study how flipping works best in each market
- Learn multiple exit strategies
- Consider when it is time to hold versus flip

12

LIABILITY ISSUES

While you need not let legal issues scare you away from going gung ho into real estate, you need to be aware of these issues. Real estate is a high-risk business, particularly when dealing with motivated sellers in foreclosure and when dealing with rehab projects. There are a lot of ways to mess up a deal and lose not just your investment but potentially more if someone has a good lawyer.

We live in a litigious society where many people seek to place blame on others. Some people believe if you treat people right and carry sufficient insurance, you will be fine. That naïve thinking can get you into a lot of trouble, and one silly lawsuit can ruin everything you've worked hard for.

KNOW THE LAW

Start by knowing the law. The old expression "Ignorance of the law is no defense" is surely true. You are expected to know the law as it applies to your business. If your state, county, city, or village has particular laws, codes, and regulations, you must learn them. Discuss your business practices regularly with a local attorney. Review your forms, agreements, and contracts to make sure the disclosures and clauses are appropriate for the particular way you do business. Although the practices described herein are generally legal and appropriate in all 50 states (and many foreign jurisdictions), if you tweak one little element in a contract, you may change the entire contract's legitimacy. An investment in good legal advice and forms is an investment in protection from future legal disasters.

CARRY LOTS OF INSURANCE

We suggest insuring each property you buy with plenty of liability coverage. You may even consider a "builder's risk" policy if you do a lot of rehab projects. If you are concerned about cost, get insurance with a large liability portion and a high deductible. If you carry your property liability, personal residence, and business insurance with a single carrier, this company will offer you an umbrella policy for several million dollars of additional coverage at a reasonable price. However, certain claims, such as breach of contract, discrimination, and misrepresentation, are not covered by insurance. In fact, most insurance won't cover any intentional act so, while having insurance is a good thing, it's only your first line of defense to lawsuits.

NEVER DO BUSINESS IN YOUR OWN NAME

You cannot expect to reduce your risk of getting sued to zero, but you can take steps to reduce your risk as much as possible. In any situation where your money is at risk, ask yourself, "Is there a better way?" Know the legal and financial risks of the situations in which you place yourself, your business, your family, and your assets.

Avoid Being a Sole Proprietor

Most people starting their own businesses do so as sole proprietors. This means they are doing business as individuals or under fictitious names or d/b/as (doing business as). This scenario offers absolutely no protection, not to mention poor tax benefits. (See Chapter 13.) If your business gets sued, all your personal assets are at risk when you are a sole proprietor. If you are the buyer or seller on a real estate contract, you (not your fictitious d/b/a) will be sued in the case of a breach of contract. If you sign a warranty deed as seller and any problems arise with the title, you can be sued for breach of warranty. If workers are injured on your property while you are rehabbing it, say hello to their lawyer. The fact is, dozens of scenarios can lead to liability, and you are fully exposed by doing things in your own name.

The best way to protect yourself is to avoid getting sued personally—that is, form a legal entity to wedge between yourself and the liabilities that your business creates. This could be a corporation or limited liability company (LLC).

Set Up a Corporation or LLC for Flipping Properties

For less than $100 in most states, you can form a corporation or limited liability company (LLC) to do your business or trade. If properly maintained, a corporation or LLC will shield your personal assets if the business gets sued or goes bankrupt. A corporation can also provide you with some tax benefits. (See the tax section in Chapter 13.) Furthermore, a corporation or LLC gives you a more professional look when dealing with people in business. A corporation can be formed with a single owner, as can an LLC, although an LLC with just one owner will be treated as a sole proprietor for federal income tax purposes, which can be detrimental if you are a dealer, also discussed in the next chapter.

What's the Difference Between an LLC and a Corporation?

Both a corporation and an LLC are formed under state law by filing papers with your state department of corporations or secretary of state. Both limit the liability of their owners but are taxed differently. You should discuss appropriate tax issues with your CPA or tax advisor before proceeding. For more information on using different entities for real estate investments, pick up a copy of *Wealth Protection Secrets of a Millionaire Real Estate Investor* (Dearborn Trade Publishing, 2003).

The best news is that you can learn to do it yourself without spending thousands of dollars in legal fees. Visit http://www.legalwiz.com and order the home study program, "How to Create a Bulletproof Corporation."

Is It Ethical to Limit Your Liability?

Some people may think that incorporating your business to limit your financial exposure is somehow unethical. Others think that lawsuits are the equivalent of legal extortion. Whether to limit your liability is a call you'll have to make. But if you do incorporate your business, you will have greater protection.

DON'T PUT REAL ESTATE IN YOUR OWN NAME

You wouldn't walk around with a financial statement taped to your forehead, would you? So why would you have your most valuable assets exposed to public scrutiny? Owning real estate in your own name is like walking around with a giant "Kick Me" sign taped to your back. In every county in the United States, copies of deeds to real estate are recorded in the public records. Anyone can go to the county courthouse or recorder's office and look up the owner of any property.

Even if you just flip properties, your name will continue to appear on public record, leaving an easy paper trail for everyone to follow. While a corporation will protect you from liability, it will not keep your affairs private. If you value privacy in today's information age, consider doing business discreetly. Even if you do everything above board, there's a good chance someone will want to tear you down, whether it is a newspaper reporter, an overzealous government agency, or an idealist plaintiff's lawyer. The lower profile you keep, the less likely you will show up on their radar screen.

Consider holding title to every property you purchase, even the ones you flip, in a land trust. A land trust (aka "Illinois Land Trust") is a revocable living trust used to hold title to property. A trustee is appointed who is a "dummy" (in legal terms, a nominee) to hold title for your benefit. The trustee cannot reveal the identity of the beneficial owner of the trust unless the trustee is brought into court and forced to by a judge. The land trust requires no filing fees, no attorney's fees, and no tax reporting, so it is inexpensive and easy to use. We suggest holding title to property in a separate trust, so it will be difficult for the public (especially lawyers) to follow your trail.

Learn to set up a land trust yourself without spending thousands of dollars in legal fees. Visit http://www.legalwiz.com and order "Step by Step Guide to Land Trusts."

DOING BUSINESS WITH PARTNERS

Doing business with a partner can be even worse than doing business as a sole proprietor. A partnership is formed when two or more people decide to do business together for profit. It does not require a formal partnership agreement or filing any official documents, although it is often formed that way. A partnership can be created even if you did not intend to, as explained below.

Here is the problem with partnerships: if your partner does something foolish, you are liable. If you allow your partner to commit the partnership to a contract, the partnership and its partners can be held liable for that debt. If your partner slanders someone, commits a negligent act, or incurs a debt on behalf of the partnership, you are on the hook—even if your partner files for bankruptcy. This is the doctrine of "joint and several liability." Regardless of the percentage of fault between you and your partners, a judgment by a creditor for any tortious acts is 100 percent collectible from any one of the partners. Joint and several liability can be particularly disastrous if you are the silent partner with all the money.

Another problem is the accidental partnership. For instance, Harry finds a good business deal. He needs capital, so he approaches Fred. Fred agrees to invest with Harry. Fred is the silent partner. Harry deals with the public, referring to his "partner" Fred. Fred and Harry do business, make money, and part ways. A month later, Harry gets into financial trouble. Creditors come knocking on his door, but he has no money to pay them. So these creditors come after his partner Fred. Is Fred liable? The answer may be yes, if the public thought Harry and Fred were partners and Fred did nothing to stop Harry.

If you only want to do a one-shot deal with a partner, consider drafting a joint venture agreement. (See the sample Joint Venture Agreement in Appendix C.) A joint venture is basically a partnership for a specific purpose. If you intend to do business with partners for the long term, consider forming a limited liability company (LLC) or limited partnership.

You can set up an LLC or limited partnership without incurring thousands of dollars in legal fees. Visit http://www.legalwiz .com and order the home study program, "How to Create Your Own Limited Liability Company or Family Limited Partnership."

KEY POINTS TO REMEMBER

- Protect yourself with adequate insurance
- Avoid doing business in your own name or as a sole proprietor
- Partners can cause liability—consider forming a corporation, an LLC, or a limited partnership

13

TAX ISSUES INVOLVED IN FLIPPING PROPERTIES

The foolish entrepreneur is the one who waits until April 15th to file taxes, then hands a shoebox full of receipts to the accountant. Be sure to plan for your taxes at the beginning of the tax year and consult with your tax advisors throughout the year. People who say the tax system isn't fair are just ignorant of the rules. Taxes will eat up a large percentage of your money over your lifetime, so learn how to make the rules work for you.

BASIC TAXATION RULES OF REAL ESTATE TRANSACTIONS

Many people wrongly assume that flipping properties causes an investor to incur a tax "penalty" or other negative tax consequences. This assessment is not completely accurate. If you buy an investment property and hold it for 12 months or more, it is considered a long-term capital asset. When sold, a long-term capital asset results in a long-term capital gain (or loss). The long-term capital gains tax rate as of January 2006 is at most 15 percent, less depending on your income. This rate is obviously lower than regular personal income tax rates, which can be as high as 35 percent.

If you held the property as a rental and took depreciation, the depreciation is "recaptured" at sale, resulting in a gain. The depreciation recapture is taxed at 25 percent. And these are just federal taxes; don't forget about state income taxes! Some states charge additional gains tax on the profit, giving a lower rate for long-term investments. Most states charge a documentary transfer tax based on purchase price, but this is the equivalent of a sales tax and is generally paid by the buyer.

Tax Issues for the Scout

The scout essentially sells information, not property, so a scout's income is treated the same as a real estate commission for income tax purposes. It would be reported as ordinary income on Schedule C of the scout's federal income tax return. The scout can deduct expenses related to this activity on the return to offset the income.

What Kind of Deductions?

You may take a lot of different business deductions, such as travel, automobile expenses, education (such as this book or a seminar), and meals (stopping for fast food while scouting around for properties).

Tax Issues for the Dealer and Retailer

The dealer who assigns a contract is not selling real estate but rather a contract, which is a commodity. This would be reported as ordinary income on Schedule C of the dealer's federal income tax return. The dealer can deduct expenses related to this activity on the tax return to offset the income.

Dealers who sell properties by double closing are selling real estate. Because each property is held less than one year, the property is not a long-term capital asset. Dealers who only sell a few properties here and there can report this income on Schedule D of their income tax return as a short-term capital gain. They can deduct expenses directly related to the acquisition and sale of the property. They cannot, however, deduct general business expenses on Schedule D. These must be reported on a Schedule C. This may open a Pandora's box, as discussed later in this chapter.

A Flipper Cannot Do a 1031 Exchange

Under section 1031 of the Internal Revenue Code, an investor who holds a property for "productive use" (with the intent to hold as an income-producing property or investment) can sell a property and replace it with another and defer paying gains tax. There are strict rules you must follow under the 1031 exchange rules. (Learn more at http://www.1031x.com.) However, a flipper can never exchange property, because the intent in buying the property would be for immediate resale, thus negating the productive use requirement. Some investors have done it, but as the saying goes, "Every tax strategy works until you get audited."

File IRS Form 1099

If you pay a scout for information or a dealer for an assignment of contract more than $600 in one year, you must send that individual an IRS Form 1099 by January 31 of the following tax year. Also, send a copy of the forms to the IRS, along with IRS Form 1096, by February 28. Failure to file the required form could result in a penalty of $50 per unfilled return or $100 if the non-filing is proven to be intentional.

If the seller takes a promissory note for all or part of the purchase price, the seller can elect to use the installment sales method under Internal Revenue Code Section 453. By using the installment method, the seller can spread out the tax on the profits over several years. In this fashion, the gain is taxed pro rata as it is received. An installment sale is defined under the Internal Revenue Code (also called the Code or IRC) as a disposition of property in which the seller receives one or more payments after the close of the tax year in which the sale occurred. Installment sales are reported on IRS Form 6252.

THE REAL ESTATE DEALER ISSUE

In Chapter 1, we specifically referred to the dealer as someone who buys properties with the intent of reselling them. The IRS uses a similar definition of a real estate dealer. The capital gains and installment sales rules apply for principal residences and properties held for productive use (IRC §1234).

If you are actively buying and selling real estate on a regular basis, you may be considered a dealer in real estate properties. A dealer is one who buys with the intent of reselling rather than for investment. In our terms, this applies to both the dealer and the retailer. There is no magic formula for determining who is an investor and who is a dealer, but the IRS will balance a number of factors, such as:

- the purpose for which the property was purchased,
- how long the property was held,
- the number of sales by the taxpayer in that year,
- the amount of income from sales compared to the taxpayer's other income,
- how many deals the taxpayer made in that year, and
- the amount of gain realized from the sale.

If the IRS pegs you as a dealer, then you cannot use the installment sales method under IRC §453. The installment sales will be disallowed, and the entire paper profit is reported as ordinary income in the year of sale. Furthermore, the sale of property cannot be reported on Schedule D; it must be reported on Schedule C as inventory. Thus the gains from the sale of real estate will be subject to self-employment tax, which is currently 15.3 percent of the first $72,600. If the IRS recharacterizes this income several years after the transaction, you may also be subject to additional interest and possibly a penalty.

Avoid Schedule C

As you may have discerned by now, doing business on a Schedule C as a sole proprietor is not recommended. Why? Because your liability is unlimited, you are subject to self-employment tax on earnings, and your chances of being audited as a small business are higher than if you are incorporated.

As discussed previously, you should consider forming a corporation to buy and flip your properties. An S corporation is fine to begin with, but consider the tax benefits of a C corporation when your business gets going full-time. Have a good certified public accountant knowledgeable in real estate transactions as a key player on your team. When sourcing an accountant, make sure that professional serves many real estate clients and, ideally, owns investment real estate, too.

Don't Become Classified as a Dealer with the IRS

If you have been classified as or choose to represent yourself as a dealer to the Internal Revenue Service, then it should be clear that you will pay additional tax. If you do file a Schedule C, careful planning may help you avoid becoming classified as a dealer. Work with your tax advisor to avoid dealer status, if possible.

What Is an S Corporation?

In the United States, an S corporation files an election under subchapter S of the Code by filing IRS Form 2553. The S corporation files an informational tax return, and the profits and losses from its business flow through to the shareholders. A C corporation files a tax return and pays taxes on its profits. Distributions (called dividends) to the shareholders are taxed again on the shareholders' personal returns. Of course, a reinvestment of profits rather than a distribution will not result in double taxation. Also, corporate income tax rates are lower than personal rates, up to about $100,000. Thus, using a C corporation for flipping properties could save you money in taxes if you reinvest rather than distribute profits each year. One type of corporation is not necessarily better than the other; you need to review your personal situation with a qualified tax advisor to see what is best for you. For more information on using different entities for real estate investments, pick up a copy of *Wealth Protection Secrets of a Millionaire Real Estate Investor* (Dearborn Trade Publishing, 2003).

INDEPENDENT CONTRACTOR LIABILITY

The IRS and your state department of labor are on the look-out for employers who don't collect and pay withholding taxes, unemployment, and/or workers' compensation insurance.

If you have employees off the books, you're looking for trouble. If you get caught, you will have to pay withholding taxes and as much as a 25 percent penalty. Intentionally failing to file W-2 forms will subject you to a $100 fine per form. The fine for failing to complete Immigration and Naturalization Service (INS) Form I-9 is from $100 to $1,000 per form. The corporation will not shield you from liability in this case, either. All officers, directors, and/or responsible parties are personally liable for the taxes, and this obligation cannot be discharged in bankruptcy.

If you have people who do contract work for you on a per diem basis, they may be considered employees by the IRS. If any workers fail to pay their estimated taxes, you may still be liable for withholding. If these workers are under your control and supervision and only work for you, the IRS may consider them employees, even if you don't. If this happens, you may be liable for back taxes and penalties as described previously.

If you want to protect yourself, at a minimum you should:

- hire only contract workers who own their own corporation, or be sure to get the business card and letterhead of any unincorporated contractors you may use to be able to prove these workers are not your employees;
- require proof of insurance (liability, unemployment, and workers' compensation) in writing,
- have a written contract or an estimate on the worker's letterhead that states that the contractor will work his or her own hours and that you will have no direct supervision over the details of the work, as in the sample Independent Contractor Agreement in Appendix C;

- have letters of reference from other people for whom the contractor worked in your file to show that this person did not work solely for you; and
- file IRS Form 1099 for every worker to whom you pay more than $600 per year.

In addition to possible tax implications, an independent contractor can create liability for you if a court determines the contractor is your employee. For example, if your independent contractor is negligent and injures another person, the injured party can sue you directly. If facts show you exercised enough control over your contractor, a court may rule that this contractor is your employee for liability purposes. As you may know, an employer is vicariously liable for the acts of its employees (i.e., liable as a matter of law without proof of fault on the part of the employer). Make certain you follow these guidelines for hiring contractors, paying particular attention to the issue of control.

Finally, be aware under your state law which duties are considered inherently dangerous. These duties cannot be delegated to an independent contractor without liability on your part, regardless of whether the person you hire is considered an independent contractor or an employee.

KEEPING GOOD RECORDS

It is important to maintain good records for your property dealings, particularly the rehabs. Plan ahead, so you can document everything if you are ever audited. In addition, many businesses fail due to poor accounting practices, so doing your books the right way will help you succeed.

If you are an active flipper, tracking the expenses between properties can get confusing. An off-the-shelf accounting program such as QuickBooks® is good for this, particularly because of its ability to attribute expenses to specific properties. The key to keeping good records is to set up simple procedures you can follow. A good CPA or bookkeeper can help you set up your accounting so your records are clean and follow Generally Accepted Accounting Principles (GAAP). There are also software packages and models for real estate investors that work with QuickBooks, such as the "KISS Guide to Real Estate Accounting" available from Legalwiz Publications (http://www.legalwiz.com/kiss).

KEY POINTS TO REMEMBER

- Learn tax rules regarding real estate, especially the rules concerning dealers

- Be mindful of the legal and tax implications of hiring people

- Keep good accounting records in case of an audit

14

STARTING AND SUCCEEDING IN THE FLIPPING BUSINESS

Whether you are new to real estate or have reached a plateau, this chapter will help jump-start your real estate investing career.

SURROUND YOURSELF WITH LIKE-MINDED PEOPLE

Creative real estate is nontraditional, which means most people don't handle real estate this way. Thus, many people you speak with will tell you this method won't work. If you say you heard about this concept in a seminar or in a course you bought from a late-night television guru, they will laugh and call you gullible. Attorneys and other professionals will denounce it because it sounds too unusual. Keep in mind that these people are either threatened by their own lack of success or are looking to protect themselves.

To find like-minded people, immediately join a local real estate investment association. (A list of associations nationwide can

be found at http://www.creonline.com/clubs.htm.) People in
these associations will help you keep your thoughts in the right
place and prove that creative real estate really does work, despite
the opinions of self-proclaimed consumer advocates. If you cannot find a group, form your own mastermind group that meets
for breakfast once a week. If you don't know what a mastermind
group is, read about it in *Think & Grow Rich* by Napoleon Hill
(Aventine Press, 2004). If you've already read this book, read it
again, again, and again!

BUILD A TEAM

Don't wait until you have a deal brewing to build your team
with the right players. You'll need the following players on your
team.

Real Estate Attorney

Finding a good attorney is difficult, because most attorneys
are not investors or are unfamiliar with creative real estate transactions. Most attorneys will give you just enough advice to keep
them from getting sued, but not enough advice to show you how
to make more money out of a deal.

A good real estate attorney advises you of the risks, suggests
alternative ways of handling a transaction, and charges a reasonable fee. A poor real estate attorney either says nothing, points
out problems without offering solutions, or systematically kills
deals.

Ask other investors in your area who they use as an attorney.
When interviewing a potential attorney, ask the following questions:

- Do you own rental property?
- How many closings do you handle per year?

- What kind of unusual transactions have you dealt with recently?
- Have you conducted any foreclosures, double closings, or installment land contracts?

Get a feel for the experience and personality of the attorney. Good attorneys are worth their weight in gold.

Title or Escrow Company

A competent title or escrow company can make closings run smoothly for you. Avoid using big-name companies. Instead, find a small, local firm that caters to investors. Make sure this company understands double closings. You can usually obtain a good recommendation on a title or escrow company from other investors by joining a real estate investment group. In some states, only attorneys perform closings, which can be a blessing or a nightmare.

Tax Advisor

In our experience, most CPAs and accountants are rank amateurs when it comes to real estate transactions. Most firms hire clerical help during the tax season, so less-experienced personnel might prepare your return. Tax return preparation is the easy part of taxes; the hard (and more important) part is using good planning and aggressive strategies. Read voraciously on how to save money on taxes. Your time will be well spent. We suggest you read *The Real Estate Investor's Tax Guide* by Vernon Hoven (Dearborn Real Estate Education, 2005).

Choose an accountant, CPA, or tax lawyer who can expertly help you plan your business taxes for the year. Consult whenever you have questions about an unusual transaction. Once you have the advice you need, consider doing your own return using a computer program, such as TurboTax by Intuit.

Good Contractor or Handy Person

A capable all-around contractor or handy person is essential to your success, especially if you don't have extensive rehab knowledge. You can find this person by looking in the "Services Directory" of your newspaper. Interview several people to find one who will give you free estimates and knows how to cut corners in all the right places. Also, ask other local investors for a recommendation.

Mortgage Broker

As a dealer, you won't need to borrow money. Once you start retailing, however, you may need cash to fund your deals. Be careful to find a mortgage broker who is savvy, creative, and experienced in working with investors.

Partner or Mentor

While this book is an excellent resource for getting started in flipping properties, it is not an exhaustive reference for every situation. You'll benefit from having partners and mentors to work with on your deals. After all, cookie cutter deals are rare; every situation is unique. The more you can tap into other people's knowledge and experience, the fewer mistakes you will make.

If you start out as a part-time investor, you can probably find a partner to be involved in your projects. This partner may already have a rehab property you can assist with, or perhaps you can team up with a contractor or another investor to help with a property you find. Either way, look at your first projects as an apprenticeship that allows you to "earn while you learn."

Look for a knowledgeable and trustworthy mentor. The investment business should be approached with integrity; most of the people who continue to succeed do business in an ethical way. Finally, don't be a leech for information. Respect other people's time and be willing to pay for it.

To continue your real estate education, check out the e-coaching program at http://www.legalwiz.com.

ONLY TALK TO MOTIVATED SELLERS

This point may seem repetitive, but it is important. Talking to sellers who are marginally motivated is the biggest mistake beginning investors can make. They waste too much time. Even worse, they drive by the house and look for comps without even talking to the seller first.

Never leave your home before speaking with a seller over the telephone. Gather as much information as you can, asking the six basic questions: who, what, where, when, how, and why? Listen for clues. Sellers won't always tell you what they really want, so you have to dig a little and be patient.

BE PERSISTENT

Anyone who has ever been in sales will tell you that few deals are ever made on the first try. In fact, most deals are made after contacting a prospect for the fourth or fifth time. Never underestimate the value of hard work. Diligence is a key to success, regardless of your background.

Employ a follow-up system for potential deals. Consider using a contact-management software program to help you schedule follow-up phone calls and action items. It also keeps a running history of calls and conversations. Microsoft Outlook works well in conjunction with a hand-held PDA or personal digital assistant. If you don't (or won't) use a computer, buy a package of index cards. Write information on each card about the property, its owners, and conversations you have had with them. Stick them on a bulletin board as follow-up reminders. No matter how you do it, just remember to follow up.

Persistence Pays

When we were conducting a real estate seminar, the camera person videotaping it told us about a colleague who might be motivated to sell. This person had bought a house, gutted it, and never finished it. He had been living in a trailer in the backyard of the house for several years. This guy was, to say the least, a real procrastinator. We called him every week. It took nearly a year of prodding to get him to sign a contract for a deal. We finally closed, rehabbed, and sold the property for over $30,000 profit. Persistence pays off!

TREAT REAL ESTATE AS A BUSINESS

People are lured into real estate because of the quick buck it promises, but don't hold your breath. You won't get rich quick. An "overnight sensation" takes about five years. More than 90 percent of the people who take a real estate seminar actually quit the real estate business after three months, suggesting that the business isn't easy. Treat flipping properties as a serious career. It takes months, even years, for a business to cultivate customers and create a life of its own. You need to treat flipping like any other business.

Don't just wander around looking for deals. Draw up a plan and follow it. Make X number of telephone calls a week. Spend X dollars a month on advertising. Make X number of offers a week. Pass out X number of business cards each day. Eventually, you will start to "get lucky." Ironically, luck always happens to those who are at the right place at the right time. If you plan and persist, you will get lucky.

SHOULD YOU INVEST IN REAL ESTATE FULL-TIME?

Many self-acclaimed real estate gurus state that people should quit their jobs and immediately jump into full-time real estate investing. They often claim incredible results from students with little experience. We would like to caution that life-changing decisions are not usually simple and that full-time investing is not for everyone.

Let's discuss some pros and cons of full-time versus part-time investing.

The Full-Time Investor

Entering the real estate profession on a full-time basis offers several advantages over a part-time commitment. Being successful requires you to develop knowledge in many aspects of real estate, and more time focused on real estate leads to greater knowledge. The more you learn, the more you earn, because you need not rely on as many professional services or partners for help. You also learn to recognize a deal (or a dud) faster, which gives you more time to do more business or to spend with your family.

As a full-time investor, you work your own hours. When we say full-time, we may mean as little as 20 hours a week if you are good at finding deals. The rest of your time can be spent pursuing other vocations or hobbies. Or, if you are so inspired, you can work 40 or more hours and use the extra cash flow to buy rental properties or diversify your holdings in the stock market. The point is that you must satisfy your cash flow needs before you can start investing your money.

One final point you should consider is whether you want to be self-employed. If you have always worked for someone else, being your own boss sounds very attractive. In some respects, this isn't quite the truth. Being your own boss means being an accountant, bookkeeper, stock clerk, receptionist, and office manager all in

one. You have to deal with tax returns, payroll, office supplies, customer service, bills, and all the other hassles that come with a business. You don't have friends to chat with at the water cooler. You
don't have paid health insurance, a company car, and a 401(k). You
take your problems home with you every night.

Sound like fun? It is, once you learn how to manage your time
and run your business. Being the master of your own life and
career is well worth the other hassles of dealing with your own
business.

The Part-Time Investor

The part-time investor holds a regular job. This may be by
choice or only for the time being, until real estate ventures bring
in enough cash to enable quitting the day job. If you can relate to
the latter reason, don't quit your job because the real estate guru
told you so. Quit your job when it is not worth the income that it
brings you. In other words, if you are making more money per
hour flipping properties on the side, you are at the point where
your regular job is costing you money. Only then is it time to quit.

One of the advantages of starting out part time is that you can
maintain your cash flow while learning the business. It may take
weeks or possibly months to find your first deal. That same deal
may take several months to turn around, especially if you decide
to fix it and sell it retail. Think twice before telling your boss
you're leaving; you will have plenty of time to make the career
switch once you have acquired more real estate experience. You
may, on the other hand, enjoy your occupation. If so, continue to
work at it and invest in real estate on the side.

The best-case scenario, if you are married, is for one spouse
to work a regular job. The other spouse works the real estate business to create wealth, retirement income, and a college fund for
the children. Of course, in today's market, you could be laid off
due to unforeseen circumstances. If you earn additional income

flipping houses and invest the proceeds in rental properties, you will have money coming in even if your main income is lost. This is especially the case for married women who often forgo careers outside the home to raise families, only to find themselves divorced with no means of making a living. We don't want to sound cynical about marriage, but with a 50 percent divorce rate in America, it never hurts to have a system for making money.

Someone with a full-time job tends to have little free time to focus on real estate. A part-timer should learn most of the same skills as a full-timer. Thus, the key disadvantage to flipping properties on a part-time basis is learning that the business takes sacrifice. Something has to give—television, lazy weekends, hobbies, and even some family activities. As with any education, time spent learning about real estate will bring its own rewards, especially if the people in your life understand your goals and your plan to achieve these goals. If you are married, make sure your spouse reads this material with you and participates in the fun process of making money.

KEEP UP YOUR EDUCATION

"If you think education is expensive, try ignorance." We are not sure who first said this, but we agree with the premise. If you think a particular book, home-study course, or training is expensive, ask yourself, "Compared to what?" You will lose more money with a mistake than you will by learning how to avoid one.

Remember, any time you spend studying is time well spent. Don't buy something just to use it as a paperweight that collects dust. No matter what the price of a book, seminar, or training program, it is always worthwhile if you put it to use and make money. However, the corollary to this statement is also true: a $20 book is a waste of money if you don't apply anything you learn from it (or if you don't ever read it!)

Are Real Estate Seminars Worth the Money?

If you read or listen to the news, you'll see a proliferation of new real estate gurus and seminars coming around to feed the endless demand for lessons about real estate. One event recently attracted more than 30,000 people, with Donald Trump as the headliner. (What does "The Donald" know about buying a duplex?)

How do you distinguish a worthwhile seminar from one that is "bad"—wastes time, offers little information, or provides misinformation? We believe there is little truly bad information out there. The difference in seminars is mainly in price and quality of the information provided.

Consider these seven points when determining whether to invest in a real estate seminar.

1. *Price.* Be leery of both very cheap and very expensive seminars. If the seminar is free, it's because the promoter wants to sell you something. It costs the promoter thousands of dollars to get people into a room, so expect a hard sales pitch. If the event is more than $1,000 per day, you should also be concerned, unless the admission price includes follow-up training or substantial reference or learning materials. So $5,000 boot camps are not all bad; just make sure you will get what you pay for.

2. *Class size.* If you are paying $5,000 for a boot camp, you should expect a small class size. If not, you are likely overpaying, because you won't be able to ask many questions in a large group.

3. *Teaching ability.* Some gurus are knowledgeable but can't teach well. Make sure you have heard the speaker before or ask other people who have attended. Nothing is worse than paying to listen to a boring speaker or someone who can't convey a topic in "plain English."

4. *Value.* Let's face it, some products are expensive because you believe they are worth more. Good marketing can make you believe Bayer is better than generic aspirin. Before you pay thousands of dollars for the brand name seminar, look into cheaper versions that aren't being marketed on TV.

5. *Pitch.* As a rule, the cheaper the seminar, the greater the pitch for other products. But some promoters do nothing but pitch, even at $5,000 boot camps. Ask others who have attended the promoter's seminars to determine the teaching-to-pitch ratio. Nothing's wrong with a promoter offering products and services at the less-expensive seminars, but it is insulting to hear a nonstop sales pitch when you are paying $1,000 a day or more.

6. *Refund policy.* Is there an open refund policy? This is very important. Ask up front. You should be extremely suspicious of any seminar that does not offer a refund policy.

7. *Are you serious about it?* No matter how much or how little you pay for a seminar, it's all up to you. No diet works without exercise and discipline, and no real estate investing technique works without your hard work. If you are just beginning, stay away from the expensive seminars until you are sure this business is for you. Start with seminars that cost $500 or less, and let the information sink in. Consider attending more advanced seminars after you have completed a few deals. Once you start making money, you should continue investing in your education, because your return will be well worth it.

Study hard, apply yourself, and, above all, make offers to purchase. You can't buy a property by studying everything about it. Too many people suffer from analysis paralysis when approaching a potential deal; they spend so much time going over minute details that they fail to take action. If you look at a potential real estate deal long enough, you will find enough reasons to talk yourself out of it for fear of losing your money. Of course, risk exists in every venture, but don't procrastinate forever. Take a chance and just do it!

KEY POINTS TO REMEMBER

- Treat real estate like a business—follow a plan

- Be persistent in following up on leads

- Assemble a team of experts

- Engage a mentor

- Keep educated, then complement your studies by taking action

A

GOOD DEAL CHECKLIST

f you answer no to one or two of the questions below, then carefully reconsider purchasing the selected property. If you answer no to three of these questions, then definitely do not do the deal. As a beginner, you should leave it for someone willing to take a large risk. As an alternative, perhaps you can sell your contract to another investor with different needs or goals.

- Would I feel safe here at night?
- Does the house fit in with others in the neighborhood?
- Is the house in a residential neighborhood (one with more houses than businesses or apartments)?
- Is the house worth saving?
- Would the house conform to FHA lending guidelines after renovations?
- Is the purchase price 25 percent less than similar homes have sold for in the neighborhood?

- Could I complete renovations in less than two months?
- Could I pay someone less than $25,000 to bring it up to satisfactory condition?
- Is the average property listed for sale in the area selling in fewer than 90 days?
- Would the house make a good starter home for a family?
- Is the block free of boarded-up houses?
- Can I fully inspect prior to closing?
- Will the owner deliver the property with a general warranty deed?

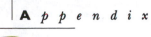

B

SAMPLE ADS

Sample Classified Ads to Buy Properties

Do You Have a Problem House?
Let us buy it and solve your
problem. We can close in as
little as 3 days.
Call Bill @ 303-555-5555

PROPERTY NOT SOLD?
We'll Make You an Offer Right
Over the Phone! We are not
Real Estate Agents.
Call Bob @ 303-555-5555

<u>*Sample Classified Ads to Sell Properties*</u>

> **FIXER PROPERTY FOR SALE**
> **All cash terms. Serious**
> **investors only.**
> **Call Bob @ 303-555-5555**

<u>*Sample Business Cards*</u>

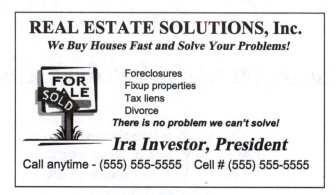

WE BUY HOUSES CASH
FAST CLOSING - AS LITTLE AS 72 HOURS
ANY CONDITION   ANY AREA

Real Estate Solutions, Inc.
Ira Investor, President
(555)555-5555

Sample Marketing Postcards

Cash for Your House
No Brokers, No Banks, No B.S.!

Closing in as Little as 72 Hrs.
We are Not Real Estate Agents
Call (555) 555-5555

DO YOU NEED TO SELL YOUR PROPERTY FAST?

Is your property vacant or in need of repairs? Are you behind in payments? Do you have back taxes owed or other liens? Do you need cash right away?

Call Us Today! Guaranteed Offer Over the Phone.
Real Estate Solutions, Inc.
Ira Investor, President
(555) 555-5555

Sample Flyer

Sample Door Hanger

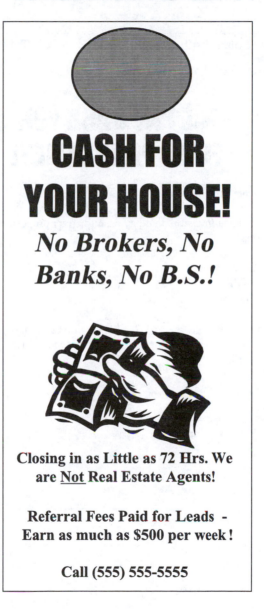

Sample Marketing Fax to Real Estate Agents

Real Estate Solutions, Inc.   Tel (555) 555-5555
123 Main Street   (555) 555-5555
Anywhere, USA12345

WE PAY CASH FOR
FIXER PROPERTIES!

Dear Real Estate Professional:

We are independent investors that pay cash for fixer properties in the following areas:

       East Side
       West Side
       Roaring Fork

We can close quickly and for ALL CASH. If you come across fixer properties in any of these areas, please call or fax the information to us and we will make an offer.

Thank you for your time.

Ira Investor, President
Real Estate Solutions, Inc.

SAMPLE FORMS

Form Name	When to Use
Standard Contract	Pro-buyer contract when dealing with for-sale-by-owner
Addendum to Contract	Pro-buyer addendum to use with standard real estate contract. Not necessary when using the standard contract.
Assignment of Contract	To assign your purchase contract to another investor
Authorization to Release Loan Information	Written permission to contact seller's lender for payoff information on a loan
Power of Attorney	Limited power of attorney for dealing with property that was quit-claimed to you in foreclosure
CYA Form	Have seller sign when you take a deed subject to an existing loan
Memorandum of Agreement	Affidavit used to cloud title to property to prevent seller from selling the property to someone else
Fax Offer	Sample fax offer to agent before contract
Quitclaim Deed	Give one whenever possible; it gives no warranty
Warranty Deed	Get one whenever possible; it has full warranties
Grant Deed	Used in California instead of a warranty deed
Appraisal Form	Excerpt from Uniform Residential Appraisal Report used by appraisers to determine value of property
Independent Contractor Agreement	Have all contractors you hire sign this form
Joint Venture Agreement	Used when doing a one-time partnership on a deal

AGREEMENT FOR PURCHASE
& SALE OF REAL ESTATE

AGREEMENT dated this <u>1st</u> day of <u>   Feb   </u> 20 <u>06</u> by and between

Mickey Motivated Seller

hereinafter "Seller" whose address is 123 Main St, Denver, CO 80203

and Real Estate Solutions, Inc.

hereinafter "Buyer" (and/or assigns or nominees) whose address is
Post Office Box 221, Denver, CO 80203

    1. <u>THE PROPERTY</u>. The parties hereby agree that Seller will sell and Buyer will buy the following property, located in and situate in the County of <u>Denver</u> , State of <u>Colorado</u> , to wit:

Lot 21, Block 12, Brighton Subdivision #1, City & County of Denver

known by street and address as <u>123 Main Street, Denver, CO 80203</u>

The sale shall also include all personal property and fixtures, except

Unless specifically excluded, all other items will be included, whether or not affixed to the property or structures. Seller expressly warrants that property, improvements, building or structures, the appliances, roof, plumbing, heating and/or ventilation systems are in good and working order. This clause shall survive closing of title.

    2. <u>PURCHASE PRICE</u>. The total purchase price to be paid by Buyer will be $<u>150,000.00</u> payable as follows:

Non-refundable earnest money deposit (see below)	$ 1,500.00
Balance due at closing	$ 149,500.00
Owner financing from seller (see below)	$ 10,000.00
New loan (see below)	$ 139,500.00
Subject to existing loans	$ N/A

Said price is subject to appraisal by buyer and/or agent of buyer's choice.

    3. <u>EARNEST MONEY</u>. The buyer's earnest money shall be held in escrow by agent of buyer's choice. Upon default of this agreement, seller shall retain earnest money as his **sole** remedy without further recourse between the parties.

4. <u>NEW LOAN</u>. This agreement is contingent upon buyer's ability to obtain a new loan in the amount of $ 139,500.00   .   Buyer is not required to accept any loan with interest rate exceeding 8   % amortized over 30   years or pay any closing costs or points exceeding $3,000   .   Buyer shall provide seller with written proof of a loan commitment on or before Feb 25   , 2006.

5. <u>SELLER FINANCING</u>. Buyer shall execute a promissory note in the amount of $ 10,000.00   . In case of default, recourse shall be against the property an there shall be no personal recourse against the borrower. As security for performance of the promissory note, buyer shall provide the seller a mortgage, deed of trust or other customary security agreement which shall be subordinate to a new first mortgage not to exceed $ 140,000.00   .

6. <u>EXISTING LOAN</u>. In the event part of the purchase price is to be satisfied by buyer taking subject to existing financing, buyer shall not be required to pay fees exceeding $ 100.00   nor be required to show income or creditworthiness to the holder of said mortgage or deed of trust. Seller expressly agrees and understands that buyer is taking the property "subject to" such mortgages or deeds of trust, and is not expressly assuming responsibility for the underlying loans. If the actual loan balance of said loan is less than as stated herein, the purchase price shall be reduced to reflect the difference; if the actual loan balance is more than as stated herein, then buyer's required cash payment shall be reduced accordingly. Seller agrees to waives tax and insurance escrows held by said lender or its/assigns.

7. <u>CLOSING</u>. Closing will held be on or about March 15   , 20 06 , at a time and place designated by buyer. Buyer shall choose the escrow, title and/or closing agent. Seller agrees to convey title by a general warranty deed.

At closing, Buyer shall pay the following costs in transferring title:

[ ] title insurance policy   [ ] loan assumption   [ ] transfer fee [✓] transfer taxes [✓] recording fees [ ] title company closing, escrow and delivery charges [ ] hazard insurance premium [ ] mortgage insurance premium [ ] survey [ ] credit application.

The following Items will be prorated at closing:
[ ] Mortgage insurance [✓] Property taxes [ ] PMI Insurance [ ] Hazard insurance
[✓] Homeowner's association dues [✓] Rents [ ] Other _____

The buyer may extend the closing date an additional THIRTY (30) days by paying the seller $ 500.00   in cash. Seller agrees to provide possession of the property free of all debris and in "broom clean" condition at closing. Buyer reserves the right to do a final "walk through" the day of closing.

8. <u>POSSESSION</u>. Seller shall surrender possession to the property in broom clean condition, and free of all personal items and debris on or before March 15 , 20 06   ("possession date", In the event possession is not delivered at closing, buyer shall withhold proceeds from the sale in the amount of $ 700.00   as security. Seller shall be liable for damages in the amount of

$ _75.00_ per day for each day the property is occupied beyond the possession date. This paragraph shall survive the closing of title.

    9. <u>EXECUTION IN COUNTERPARTS</u>. This agreement may be executed in counterparts and by facsimile signatures. This agreement shall become effective as of the date of the last signature.

    10. <u>INSPECTION</u>. This agreement is subject to the final inspection and approval of the property by the buyer in writing on or before ___March 15___, 20_06_.

    11. <u>ACCESS</u>. Buyer shall be entitled a key and be entitled to access to show partners, lenders, inspectors and/or contractors prior to closing. Buyer may place an appropriate sign on the property prior to closing for prospective tenants and/or assigns.

Mickey Motivated Seller   *Feb 1, 2006*
_____   _____
Seller   Date

_____   _____
Seller   Date

Real Estate Solutions, Inc. by
Ira Investor, President   *Feb 1, 2006*
_____   _____
Buyer   Date

STATE OF *Colorado*   )
) ss:
COUNTY OF *Denver*   )

On   *Feb 1st*___, 20 *06* , before me, *Nancy Notary*___, a notary public in and for said state personally appeared *Mickey Motivated Seller*___, personally known to me (or proved to me based upon satisfactory evidence) to be the person(s) whose name(s) are subscribed to the within instrument and acknowledged that (s)he/they executed the same in his/her/their signature on the instrument the person(s) or entity on behalf of which they acted, executed the instrument.

Witness my hand and official seal

                                         NOTARY SEAL

Nancy Notary
_____
NOTARY PUBLIC
My commission expires *Jan 15, 2008*___

CONTRACT ADDENDUM

Addendum to contract dated _____Feb_____ __1st__ , 20__06__

Property Address: __123 Main Street. Denver. CO 80203__

Seller(s) __Mickey Motivated Seller__

Buyer(s) __Real Estate Solutions, Inc.__

Notwithstanding anything to the contrary in the attached contract, the parties agree as follows:

EARNEST MONEY. The buyer's earnest money shall be held in escrow by agent of buyer's choice. Upon default of this agreement, seller shall retain earnest money as his sole remedy without further recourse between the parties.

SELLER FINANCING. In the event of any Seller financing, the promissory Note to be executed by the Buyer shall have no personal recourse against the borrower.

EXISTING LOAN. In the event part of the purchase price is to be satisfied by buyer taking subject to existing financing, buyer shall not be required to pay fees exceeding $ 100.00_____ nor be required to show income or creditworthiness to the holder of said mortgage or deed of trust. Seller expressly agrees and understands that buyer is taking the property "subject to" such mortgages or deeds of trust, and is not expressly assuming responsibility for the underlying loans. If the actual loan balance of said loan is less than as stated herein, the purchase price shall be reduced to reflect the difference; if the actual loan balance is more than as stated herein, then buyer's required cash payment shall be reduced accordingly. Seller agrees to waives tax and insurance escrows held by said lender or its/assigns.

The buyer may extend the closing date an additional THIRTY (30) days by paying the seller $__500.00_____in cash. Buyer reserves the right to do a final "walk through" the day of closing.

POSSESSION. Seller shall surrender possession to the property in broom clean condition, and free of all personal items and debris on or before _March 15___ , 20__06__ ("possession date"). In the event possession is not delivered at closing, buyer shall withhold proceeds from the sale in the amount of $_700.00_____ as security. Seller shall be liable for damages in the amount of $ 75.00__ per day for each day the property is occupied beyond the possession date. This paragraph shall survive the closing of title.

EXECUTION IN COUNTERPARTS. This agreement may be executed in counterparts and by facsimile signatures. This agreement shall become effective as of the date of the last signature.

INSPECTION. This agreement is subject to the final inspection and approval of the property by the buyer in writing on or before _____March 15_____ , 20__06___ .

ACCESS. Buyer shall be entitled a key and be entitled to access to show partners, lenders, inspectors and/or contractors prior to closing. Buyer may place an appropriate sign on the property prior to closing for prospective tenants and/or assigns.

Mickey Motivated Seller   *Feb 1, 2006*
_____   _____
Seller   Date

_____   _____
Seller   Date

Real Estate Solutions, Inc. by
Ira Investor, President   *Feb 1, 2006*
_____   _____
Buyer   Date

ASSIGNMENT OF CONTRACT

Real Estate Solutions, Inc. _____(hereinafter "Assignor"), the Buyer under an

agreement dated_____Feb_____1st_, 20____06____ (hereinafter "Agreement") by and between

Assignor and _Mickey Motivated Seller_____(hereinafter "Seller"), hereby assigns

all right, title and interest in said agreement to_Ronnie Retailer_____

(hereinafter "Assignee") for the sum and consideration of $_3,500.00_____

received by Assignor.

     Assignee agrees to perform all covenants, conditions and obligations required by
Assignor under said Agreement and agrees to defend, indemnify and hold Assignor harmless
from any liability or obligation under said Agreement. Assignee further agrees to hold Assignor
harmless from any deficiency or defect in the legality or enforceability of the terms of said
agreement.

Dated this _1st_ day of _____Feb_____, 20_06_____

Real Estate Solutions, Inc. by
Ira Investor, President
_____
Assignor

Ronny Retailer
_____
Assignee

AUTHORIZATION TO RELEASE LOAN INFORMATION

Authorization dated this <u>1st</u> day of <u>Feb</u> , 20 <u>06</u>

Borrower(s): <u>Mickey Motivated Seller</u>

Loan No.: <u>1234567</u>

Property: <u>123 Main Street, Denver, CO 80203</u>

TO: <u>Northwest Mortgage, PO Box 132, Fargo, ND 65434</u>

_____

_____

I/We the undersigned hereby authorize you to release information regarding the above-referenced loan to <u>Real Estate Solutions, Inc.</u>
and/or their agents/assigns. This form may be duplicated in blank and or sent via facsimile transmission. This authorization is a continuation authorization for said persons to receive information about my loan, including duplicates of any notices sent to me regarding my loan.

Mickey Motivated Seller
_____
Borrower

DOB: <u>3/10/62</u>

SSN: <u>234-345-6787</u>

_____
Borrower

DOB: _____

SSN: _____

LIMITED POWER OF ATTORNEY

KNOW ALL MEN BY THESE PRESENTS:

THAT, I,_____Mickey Motivated Seller_____, of the County of

___Denver_____ State of _____Colorado_____, reposing special trust and

confidence in _Real Estate Solutions, Inc._____ (hereinafter "Agent"), of the County of

____Denver_____, State of _Colorado____

have made, constituted and appointed, and by these presents do make, constitute and appoint said Agent to be my true and lawful attorney-in-fact, to act for me and in my stead, and to sell and convey the following property (enter legal description below):
Lot 21, Block 12, Brighton Subdivision #1, City & County of Denver

or any interest in said land for such price as to my agent may seem advisable.

My agent is hereby authorized to sign, seal and deliver as my act and deed any contract, deed, or other instrument in execution of any agreement for sale made by me or my agent, in such manner that all my estate, right, title and interest in said land may be effectually and absolutely conveyed and assigned to the purchaser thereof, his, her, or its heirs, successors and assigns forever, or to such other person or entity as purchaser may name or appoint; and I hereby declare that any and all of the contracts, deeds, receipts or matters, and things which shall be by my said agent given, made or done for the aforesaid purposes shall be as good, valid and effectual as if they had been signed, sealed and delivered by me in my own proper person; and I hereby undertake at all times to ratify whatsoever my said agent shall lawfully do or cause to be done in or concerning the premises by virtue of these presents. My agent is hereby further authorized to receive the consideration or purchase price arising from the sale of such land or any interest therein, and to give good receipt therefore, which receipt shall exonerate the person paying such money to my agent from looking to the application, or being responsible for the loss or misapplication thereof. If said consideration should be paid by check or draft, my said agent is hereby authorized to endorse and cash said check or draft and collect the proceeds thereof, whether the same be made payable to me or to my agent, as my attorney-in-fact. My agent may contact and lender, lien holder or government authority regarding money or other obligations owed regarding the property and may further execute any and all documents necessary to correct any deficiency in previously executed documents regarding the ownership or sale of the property.

IN WITNESS WHEREOF, I have hereunto set my hand and seal this *1st* day of *February*, 20 *06*.

STATE OF *Colorado*, COUNTY OF *Denver*)ss:

Mickey Motivated Seller
_____
Principal's Name

Mickey Motivated Seller
_____
Principal's Legal Signature

On *Feb 1st*, 20 *06*, before me, *Nancy Notary*, a notary public in and for said state personally appeared
Mickey Motivated Seller,
_____personally known to me
(or proved to me based upon satisfactory evidence) to be the person(s) whose name(s) are subscribed to the within instrument and acknowledged that (s)he/they executed the same in his/her/their signature on the instrument the person(s) or entity on behalf of which they acted, executed the instrument.

Witness my hand and official seal

Nancy Notary
_____
NOTARY PUBLIC
My commission expires *Jan 15, 2008*

"DUE-ON-SALE" ACKNOWLEDGMENT

WHEREAS, ___Mickey Motivated Seller_____ as Seller and
___Real Estate Solutions, Inc._____ as Purchaser have entered in to a certain
purchase and sales agreement even date herewith, the parties fully understand, acknowledge an
agree as follows:

     1. Both Seller and Purchase are fully aware that the mortgage(s)/deeds of trust securing
the property located at ___123 Main Street, Denver, CO___ contain(s) provisions prohibiting the
transfer of any interest in the property without satisfying the principal balance remaining on the
underlying loans and/or obtaining the lender's prior written consent (i.e., a "due-on-sale" clause),
and that this transaction may violate said mortgage. **Seller specifically understands that this
loan will be paid on a monthly basis by buyer, but will not be assumed or paid off
completely at this time, and that this loan will remain in Seller's name and may continue to
appear on Seller's credit report.**

     2. Seller and Purchaser execute this disclosure form after having had the opportunity to
seek legal counsel as to the legal and financial implications of the due-on-sale clause. The
parties agree and understand that if said due on sale clause is enforced by the holders of said
mortgages, the entire balance due under said mortgages/deeds of trust will have to be paid off.
In this event, Seller and Purchaser agree to take all reasonable steps to satisfy said lender,
including both parties taking steps to obtain financing and/or Purchaser submitting an application
to formally assume liability for said obligations. Purchaser understands that in the event that the
underlying debt is not paid off, the lender holding the deeds of trust may foreclose the property
which will extinguish Purchaser's interest in the property.

     3. Seller and Purchaser hereby agreed to defend, indemnify and hold all parties involved
in this transaction harmless from any liability in the event that the holders of the mortgages
and/or deeds of trust on the aforementioned property are called due and payable.

Mickey Motivated Seller
_____   _____
Seller   Purchaser

On _**Feb 1st**___, 20 _**06**_ , before me, _**Nancy Notary**___, a notary public in and for said state personally
appeared _**Mickey Motivated Seller**___, personally known to me (or proved to me based upon satisfactory
evidence) to be the person(s) whose name(s) are subscribed to the within instrument and acknowledged that
(s)he/they executed the same in his/her/their signature on the instrument the person(s) or entity on behalf of which
they acted, executed the instrument.

Witness my hand and official seal

**Nancy Notary**
_____
NOTARY PUBLIC
My commission expires _**Jan 15, 2008**_____   [SEAL]

AFFIDAVIT AND MEMORANDUM OF AGREEMENT CONCERNING REAL ESTATE

State of _____Colorado_____)
County of ___Denver_____) ss:

BEFORE ME, the undersigned authority, on this day personally appeared

___Real Estate Solutions, Inc._____, who being first duly sworn, deposes and says

that an agreement for the Purchase and Sale of the real property described as (enter legal

description below): Lot 21, Block 12, Brighton Subdivision #1, City & County of Denver

was entered into by and between the undersigned Affiant, as Buyer, and _____

___Mickey Motivated Seller_____, as Seller, on the ___1st___ day of

_____Feb_____, 20__06___.

A copy of the agreement for purchase and sale of said real property may be obtained by

contacting ___Real Estate Solutions, Inc._____, whose mailing address is

___Post Office Box 221, Denver, CO 80203_____, and whose telephone

number is ___(555) 555-5555_____.

Dated this ___1st___ day of _____Feb_____, 20__06__.

FURTHER AFFIANT SAYETH NOT.

AFFIANT'S NAME ___Real Estate Solutions, Inc._____

AFFIANT'S SIGNATURE ___*Ira Investor*_____

On ___*Feb 1st*___, 20 _06_, before me, ___*Nancy Notary*___, a notary public in and for said
state personally appeared ___*Ira Investor*_____, personally known to me (or
proved to me based upon satisfactory evidence) to be the person(s) whose name(s) are subscribed
to the within instrument and acknowledged that (s)he/they executed the same in his/her/their
signature on the instrument the person(s) or entity on behalf of which they acted, executed the
instrument.

Witness my hand and official seal

___*Nancy Notary*_____

NOTARY PUBLIC
My commission expires ___*Jan 15, 2008*_____   [SEAL]

FAX OFFER TO PURCHASE

<u>TO</u>: Barney Broker
<u>FROM</u>: Ira Investor
<u>DATE</u>: January 29, 2006
<u>RE</u>: 1234 Main Street, Anywhere, USA, MLS Listing #12345

Dear Mr. Broker:

We are willing to submit a formal offer to purchase the above-referenced property for $110,000 cash and close on or before February 15th, 2006. This offer will expire if not accepted on or before 5:00 PM, February 1, 2006.

Please present this information verbally to your client.

Upon acceptance, we will submit a company check in the sum of $500 as earnest money and execute a formal real estate purchase contract.

This offer is subject to a complete inspection of the premises.

Ira Investor

_____
Ira Investor

-------------------------------[Space Above Reserved for Recording Purposes]------------------------

QUIT-CLAIM DEED

THIS QUIT-CLAIM DEED, is executed this ___1st___ day of ___Feb___, 20__06__ by

     Mickey Motivated Seller _____ hereinafter referred to as "First Party", to

     Real Estate Solutions, Inc. _____ hereinafter referred to as "Second Party", whose

address is __Post Office Box 221, Denver, CO 80203_____.

WITNESSETH, that the First Party, for and in consideration of the sum of $10.00 and other good and valuable consideration in hand paid by the said Second Party, the receipt whereof is hereby acknowledged, does hereby remise, release and quit-claim unto the Second Party, all right, title, interest, and claim which the First Party has in and to the following described lot, piece or parcel of land, situate, lying and being in the county of _____Denver_____, State of _____Colorado_____ to wit:

     Lot 21, Block 12, Brighton Subdivision #1, City & County of Denver

Also known as street and number as __123 Main Street, Denver, CO 80203_____.

TO HAVE AND HOLD the same, together with all and singular the appurtenances thereunto, of all interest, equity and claim whatsoever the First Party may have, either in law or equity, for the proper use, benefit and behalf of the Second Party forever.

IN WITNESS WHEREOF, the First Party has signed and sealed these presents the day and year first above written.

Mickey Motivated Seller
_____   _____
First Party   First Party

STATE OF *Colorado*____, COUNTY OF *Denver*_____)ss:

On *Feb 1st*_____, 20__06__, before me, *Nancy Notary*_____, a notary public in and for said state personally appeared *Mickey Motivated Seller*_____, personally known to me (or proved to me based upon satisfactory evidence) to be the person(s) whose name(s) are subscribed to the within instrument and acknowledged that (s)he/they executed the same in his/her/their signature on the instrument the person(s) or entity on behalf of which they acted, executed the instrument.

Witness my hand and official seal

*Nancy Notary*_____
NOTARY PUBLIC
My commission expires *Jan 15, 2008*_____   [NOTARY SEAL]

----------------------------[Space Above Reserved for Recording Purposes]------------------------

WARRANTY DEED

THIS DEED, made this __1st__ day of_____Feb_____, 20 _06_ between

_____Mickey Motivated Seller_____the grantor, and

_____Real Estate Solutions, Inc._____the grantee, whose address is
_____Post Office Box 221, Denver, CO 80203

WITNESSETH, that the grantor, for and in consideration of the sum of TEN DOLLARS ($10.00), the receipt and sufficiency of which is hereby acknowledged and received, and for other good and valuable consideration, has granted bargained, sold and conveyed, and by these presents does grant, bargain sell, convey and confirm unto the grantee, their heirs and assigns forever, all the real property, together with improvements, if any, situate and being in the County of _____Denver_____, State of ____Colorado____, described as follows:

Lot 21, Block 12, Brighton Subdivision #1, City & County of Denver

Also known as street and number _123 Main Street, Denver, CO 80203_____.

TOGETHER with all and singular hereditaments and appurtenances thereunto belonging, or in anywise appertaining and the reversion and reversions, remainder and remainders, rents, issues, and profits thereof, and all the estate, right, title, interest, claim and demand whatsoever of the said grantor, either in law or equity, of, in and to the above bargained premises, with the hereditaments and appurtenances.

TO HAVE AND TO HOLD the said premises above bargained and described, with the appurtenances, unto the said grantee, their heirs and assigns forever. And the said grantor, for himself, his heirs, and personal representatives, does covenant, grant bargain and agree to and with the grantee, their heirs and assigns, that at the time of the ensealing and delivery of these presents, is well seized of the premises above conveyed, has good, sure, perfect, absolute indefeasible estate if inheritance, in law, in fee simple, and has good right, full power and lawful authority to grant, bargain, sell and convey the same in manner and form aforesaid, and that the same are free and clear from all former and other grants, bargains, sales, liens, taxes, assessments, encumbrances and restrictions of any kind or nature whatsoever, except any easements, restrictions, covenants, zoning ordinances and rights-of-way of record and property taxes accruing subsequent to _December 31, 2005_____, a lien not yet due and payable.

The grantor shall and will WARRANT AND FOREVER DEFEND the above-bargained premises in the quiet and peaceable possession of the grantee, his heirs, and assigns, against all and every person or persons lawfully claiming the whole or any part thereof. The singular shall include the plural, the plural shall include the singular, and the use of any gender shall be applicable to all genders.

IN WITNESS WHEREOF, the grantor has executed this deed on the date set forth above.

*Mickey Motivated Seller*_____

Grantor

STATE OF_*Colorado*____, COUNTY OF_*Denver*_____)ss:

On *Feb 1st*___, 20 _06_ , before me, *Nancy Notary*_____, a notary public in and for said state personally appeared
*Mickey Motivated Seller*_____,
_____personally known to me (or proved to me based upon satisfactory evidence) to be the person(s) whose name(s) are subscribed to the within instrument and acknowledged that (s)he/they executed the same in his/her/their signature on the instrument the person(s) or entity on behalf of which they acted, executed the instrument.

Witness my hand and official seal

*Nancy Notary*_____
NOTARY PUBLIC   My commission expires _*Jan 15, 2008*_

Recording requested by

and when recorded, please return this deed
and tax statements to:
Post Office Box 221, Denver, CO 80203

For recorder's use only

CALIFORNIA GRANT DEED

[   ] This transfer is exempt from the documentary transfer tax
[X] The documentary transfer tax is $_____ and is computed on:
    [   ] the full value of the interest in the property conveyed
    [X] the full value less the value of liens of encumbrances remaining at the time of sale
The property is located in an [   ] unincorporated area. [   ] the city of Los Angeles

For a valuable consideration, receipt of which is hereby acknowledged,
Mickey Motivated Seller
hereby grant(s) to Real Estate Solutions, Inc.

the following real property in the City of Los Angeles , County of Los Angeles ,
_____state of California:

Lot 21, Block 4, Shady Acres 3rd Filing, City and County of Los
Angeles, State of California

Date: _____

                            Grantor

Date: *Feb 1, 2006*   *Mickey Motivated Seller*

                            Grantor

STATE OF *Colorado* , COUNTY OF *Denver*)ss:

On *Feb 1st* , 20 *06* , before me, *Nancy Notary* , a notary public in and for said state
personally appeared *Mickey Motivated Seller* , personally known to me (or proved to me based
upon satisfactory evidence) to be the person(s) whose name(s) are subscribed to the within instrument and
acknowledged that (s)he/they executed the same in his/her/their signature on the instrument the person(s) or entity
on behalf of which they acted, executed the instrument.

Witness my hand and official seal

Nancy Notary
_____
NOTARY PUBLIC
My commission expires *Jan 15, 2008*

                              [NOTARY SEAL]

Paul J. Piekos

Summary Appraisal Report
Property Description

UNIFORM RESIDENTIAL APPRAISAL REPORT

File No. DEMO-URAR

SUBJECT

Property Address 1234 White Eagle Drive	City Anywhere State IL Zip Code 605XX
Legal Description Lot X in White Eagle Club Unit X	County Will
Assessor's Parcel No. 01-04-101-XXX	Tax Year 1996 R.E. Taxes $ 7,564.32 Special Assessments $ 0.00
Borrower Buyn, Ima	Current Owner Seller, Homer Occupant: ☒ Owner ☐ Tenant ☐ Vacant
Property rights appraised ☒ Fee Simple ☐ Leasehold	Project Type ☒ PUD ☐ Condominium (HUD/VA only) HOA $ 65.00 /Mo.
Neighborhood or Project Name White Eagle Club	Map Reference 30W-10S Census Tract 8803.02
Sale Price $ 425,000 Date of Sale 05/29/98	Description and $ amount of loan charges/concessions to be paid by seller None known
Lender/Client XYZ Financial Inc.	Address 1234 Main Street, Anywhere, IL 605XX
Appraiser Paul J. Piekos SRA	Address 413 Braemar Av., Naperville, IL 60563

NEIGHBORHOOD

Location	☐ Urban ☒ Suburban ☐ Rural	Predominant occupancy	Single family housing	Present land use %	Land use change
Built up	☒ Over 75% ☐ 25-75% ☐ Under 25%		PRICE $(000) / AGE (yrs)	One family 80	☒ Not likely ☐ Likely
Growth rate	☒ Rapid ☐ Stable ☐ Slow	☒ Owner	180 Low 0	2-4 family	☒ In process
Property values	☐ Increasing ☒ Stable ☐ Declining	☐ Tenant	700 High 10	Multi-family 5	To: Improved Resident
Demand/supply	☐ Shortage ☒ In balance ☐ Oversupply	☒ Vacant (0-5%)	Predominant	Commercial 10	
Marketing time	☐ Under 3 mos. ☒ 3-6 mos. ☐ Over 6 mos.	☐ Vac.(over 5%)	300 5	Industrial 5	

Note: Race and the racial composition of the neighborhood are not appraisal factors.

Neighborhood boundaries and characteristics: Predominantly single family detached housing. Boundaries are New York Street east, 95th Street south, Kendall County line west.

Factors that affect the marketability of the properties in the neighborhood (proximity to employment and amenities, employment stability, appeal to market, etc.): Subject is located in a rapidly growing area in a residential neighborhood comprised mostly of custom bui quality construction. Most all the dwellings appear to project good curb appeal. Compatibility of propert neighborhood services and conveniences are average for the area. Area employment has been stable and empl present or closeby. Overall, a marketable area with good appeal to purchasers within this price range.

Market conditions in the subject neighborhood (including support for the above conclusions related to the trend of property values, demand/supply, and marketing time -- such as data on competitive properties for sale in the neighborhood, description of the prevalence of sales and financing concessions, etc.): Housing values have either held steady or increased gradually within the past twelve months. Properties us The demand for housing in the subject neighborhood is consistent with the rest of nearby competing areas, under 90 days. Homes in the subject's price range have a typical marketing time of 90-120 days. Financing market rates. Financing is usually through the conventional process with the lower end of the value range concessions necessary.

PUD

Project Information for PUDs (if applicable) -- Is the developer/builder in control of the Home Owners' Association (HOA)? ☒ Yes ☐ No
Approximate total number of units in the subject project 1100 Approximate total number of units for sale in the subject project 59
Describe common elements and recreational facilities: Clubhouse, pool, tennis courts and the common areas.

SITE

Dimensions 98 X 150 X 81 X 155	Topography Basically level
Site area Approx. 13,600 Sq.Ft.	Size Typical for the area
Specific zoning classification and description R-1A P.U.D. Single Family Residential Corner Lot ☐ Yes ☒ No	Shape Slightly irregular
Zoning compliance ☒ Legal ☐ Legal nonconforming (Grandfathered use) ☐ Illegal ☐ No zoning	Drainage Appears adequate
Highest & best use as improved: ☒ Present use ☐ Other use (explain)	View Golf course

Utilities	Public	Other	Off-site Improvements	Type	Public	Private	Landscaping Good
Electricity	☒	Underground	Street	Asphalt	☒	☐	Driveway Surface Concrete
Gas	☒		Curb/gutter	Concrete	☒	☐	Apparent easements Public utilities
Water	☒		Sidewalk	Concrete	☒	☐	FEMA Special Flood Hazard Area ☐ Yes ☒ No
Sanitary sewer	☒		Streetlights	Electric	☒	☐	FEMA Zone Zone C Map Date 05/18/92
Storm sewer	☒		Alley	None			FEMA Map No. #170213 0020C

Comments (apparent adverse easements, encroachments, special assessments, slide areas, illegal or legal nonconforming zoning use, etc.): Site consists o average sized lot with a premium location that backs to the golf course which projects good appeal. Lands readily apparent adverse easements or encroachments.

DESCRIPTION OF IMPROVEMENTS

GENERAL DESCRIPTION		EXTERIOR DESCRIPTION		FOUNDATION		BASEMENT		INSULATION	
No. of Units	One	Foundation	Poured Conc.	Slab	None	Area Sq. Ft.	1,424	Roof	☐
No. of Stories	Two	Exterior Walls	Frame/Brick	Crawl Space	Partial	% Finished	50%	Ceiling	☐
Type (Det./Att.)	Detached	Roof Surface	Asphalt Shin	Basement	Partial	Ceiling	Suspended	Walls	☐
Design (Style)	2 Story	Gutters & Dwnspts.	Aluminum	Sump Pump	Present	Walls	Drywall	Floor	☐
Existing/Proposed	Existing	Window Type	Casement	Dampness	None noted	Floor	Carpeted	None	☐
Age (Yrs.)	4	Storm/Screens	Thermalpane	Settlement	None noted	Outside Entry	None	Unknown Cncld.	☒
Effective Age (Yrs.)	2	Manufactured House	No	Infestation	None noted	200 amp service		Ceiling Fan(s)	

ROOMS	Foyer	Living	Dining	Kitchen	Den	Family Rm.	Rec. Rm.	Bedrooms	# Baths	Laundry	Other	Area Sq. Ft.
Basement							X					1,42
Level 1	X	1	1	1		1		1	1.5	X		2,26
Level 2								3	1.0			941

Finished area above grade contains: 8 Rooms; 4 Bedroom(s); 2.5 Bath(s); 3,20 Square Feet of Gross Living Area

INTERIOR	Materials/Condition	HEATING		KITCHEN EQUIP.		ATTIC		AMENITIES		CAR STORAGE	
Floors	Carpet/HW/Tile/G	Type	FWA	Refrigerator	☒	None	☐	Fireplace(s) # 1	☒	None	☐
Walls	Drywall/Good	Fuel	Gas	Range/Oven	☒	Stairs	☐	Patio Brick	☒	Garage	# of cars
Trim/Finish	Stained/Good	Condition	Good	Disposal	☒	Drop Stair	☐	Deck Wood	☒	Attached	3
Bath Floor	Ceramic/Good	COOLING		Dishwasher	☒	Scuttle	☒	Porch	☐	Detached	
Bath Wainscot	Ceramic/Good	Central	Present	Fan/Hood	☒	Floor	☐	Fence	☐	Built-In	
Doors	Six Panel/Good	Other	None	Microwave	☐	Heated	☐	Pool Whirlpool T	☒	Carpot	
Ceramic tile front entry		Condition	Good	Washer/Dryer	☒	Finished	☐	Skylights	☐	Driveway	6

Additional features (special energy efficient items, etc.): See attached addenda.

COMMENTS

Condition of the improvements, depreciation (physical, functional, and external), repairs needed, quality of construction, remodeling/additions, etc.: Subject property is in good condition, exhibiting minimal physical deterioration. Improvements are of very good qu acceptable and considered typical for this style home in this area. No functional inadequacies or externa Marketability of the property is good.

Adverse environmental conditions (such as, but not limited to, hazardous wastes, toxic substances, etc.) present in the improvements, on the site, or in the immediate vicinity of the subject property.: No visible external adverse environmental conditions were observed. No on-sit were disclosed to the appraiser at the time of inspection.

Form UA2 — "TOTAL2000 for Windows" appraisal software by a la mode, inc. — 1-800-ALAMODE

File No. DEMO-URAR Page #3

UNIFORM RESIDENTIAL APPRAISAL REPORT   File No. DEMO-URAR

Valuation Section

ESTIMATED SITE VALUE .... = $	100,00	Comments on Cost Approach (such as, source of cost estimate, site value, square foot calculation and for HUD, VA and FmHA, the estimated remaining economic life of the property): Physical depreciation is calc' using the effective age/economic life method on No significant functional obsolescence or exter was observed. Due to the lack of available vacar the allocation method was used to estimate the s is replacement cost. Figures taken from the Mar Residential Cost Handbook for a single family dv good quality construction. Estimated remaining e 68 years.

ESTIMATED REPRODUCTION COST-NEW-OF IMPROVEMENTS:

Dwelling 3,20 Sq. Ft. @$ 81.35 = $	260,40	
1,42 Sq. Ft. @$ 37.04 =	52,74	
Appliances, FP, Whirlpool, Deck =	24,10	
Garage/Carport 774 Sq. Ft. @$ 29.93 =	23,16	
Total Estimated Cost New .... = $	360,41	
Less Physical Functional External		
Depreciation 10,30 | 0 | 0 =$	10,30	
Depreciated Value of Improvements .... =$	350,11	
"As-is" Value of Site Improvements .... =$	7,07	
INDICATED VALUE BY COST APPROACH .... =$	457,18	

ITEM	SUBJECT	COMPARABLE NO. 1		COMPARABLE NO. 2		COMPARABLE NO. 3	
Address	1234 White Eagle Drive Anywhere	3607 Scottsdale Circle Anywhere		3123 Aviara Circle Anywhere		3131 Aviara Circle Anywhere	
Proximity to Subject		2 Blocks South		3 Blocks East		3 Blocks East	
Sales Price	$ 425,00	$ 418,00		$ 444,50		$ 453,00	
Price/Gross Living Area	$ 132.7	$ 123.8		$ 121.4		$ 111.6	
Data and/or	Inspection	MLS of Northern Illinois		MLS of Northern Illinois		MLS of Northern Illinois	
Verification Source	Assessor	Wheatland Twsp. Assessor		Wheatland Twsp. Assessor		Wheatland Twsp. Assessor	
VALUE ADJUSTMENTS	DESCRIPTION	DESCRIPTION	+( )$ Adjust.	DESCRIPTION	+( )$ Adjust.	DESCRIPTION	+( )$ Adjust.
Sales or Financing		Conventional		Conventional		Conventional	
Concessions		None Known		None Known		None Known	
Date of Sale/Time		11/97		2/98		7/97	
Location	Good	Similar		Similar		Similar	
Leasehold/Fee Simple	Fee Simple	Fee Simple		Fee Simple		Fee Simple	
Site	98 X 150 irre	70 X 151 irre	+10,00	119 X 150 irr		90 X 135 irre	
View	Golf Course	Golf Course		Golf Course		Golf Course	
Design and Appeal	2 Story/Good	2 Story/Equal		2 Story/Equal		2 Story/Equal	
Quality of Construction	Frame/Brick	Dryvit/Stone		Frame/Brick		Frame/Brick	
Age	4	2		2		3	
Condition	Good	Good		Good		Good	
Above Grade	Total | Bdrms | Baths	Total | Bdrms | Baths	Bath	Total | Bdrms | Baths	Bath:	Total | Bdrms | Baths	Bath:
Room Count	8 | 4 | 2.5	10 | 3 | 3.5	-2,00	9 | 4 | 4.0	-3,00	10 | 4 | 4.0	-3,00
Gross Living Area	3,20 Sq. Ft.	3,37 Sq. Ft.	-6,96	3,66 Sq. Ft.	-18,36	4,05 Sq. Ft.	-34,20
Basement & Finished	Partial	Partial		Partial		Partial	
Rooms Below Grade	50% Finished	None	+10,00	None	+10,00	None	+10,00
Functional Utility	Average	Average		Average		Average	
Heating/Cooling	GFWA/CAC	GFWA/CAC		GFWA/CAC		GFWA/CAC	
Energy Efficient Items	Skylights	Skylights		Skylights		Skylights	
Garage/Carport	3 Car Garage	3 Car Garage		3 Car Garage		3 Car Garage	
Porch, Patio, Deck,	Deck,Patio	Deck,Patio		Deck	+2,00	Deck	+2,00
Fireplace(s), etc.	1 Fireplace	1 Fireplace		2 Fireplaces	-2,50	1 Fireplace	
Fence, Pool, etc.	Whirlpool Tub	Whirlpool Tub		Whirlpool Tub		Whirlpool Tub	
Other	Security Syst	Security Syst		Security Syst		Security Syst	
Net Adj. (total)		☒ + ☐ |$	11,04	☒ + ☐ |$	11,86	☒ + ☐ |$	25,20
Adjusted Sales Price of Comparable		Net 2.5 % Gross 6.9 % $	429,04	Net 2.7 % Gross 8.1 % $	432,64	Net 5.0 % Gross 10.9 % $	427,80

Comments on Sales Comparison (including the subject property's compatibility to the neighborhood, etc.): All sales are similar custom built hom the subject subdivision. Comps #2 and #3 are located in a similar phase of the subject subdivision, Comp the lot sizes are smaller. All have similar locations that back to the golf course. All were adjusted for homes adjusted for size @ $40 per sq.ft. All lack the finished basement. All have similar amenities to th over six months old, it was the best available. A time adjustment is not necessary. Most weight was given from Comp #1.

ITEM	SUBJECT	COMPARABLE NO. 1	COMPARABLE NO. 2	COMPARABLE NO. 3
Date, Price and Data Source, for prior sales within year of appraisal	No prior sale the past 12 months per ML	No other prior sale repo the past 12 months per M public records and/or as	No other prior sale repo the past 12 months per M public records and/or as	No other prior sale repo the past 12 months per M public records and/or as

Analysis of any current agreement of sale, option, or listing of subject property and analysis of any prior sales of subject and comparables within one year of the date of appraisal: Subject property sold within 95% of the list price and within a reasonable marketing time for similar lik comparable sales used shows no other recent sales activity.

INDICATED VALUE BY SALES COMPARISON APPROACH		$ 429,00
INDICATED VALUE BY INCOME APPROACH (if Applicable) Estimated Market Rent $ N/A /Mo. x Gross Rent Multiplier N/A = $		N/A

This appraisal is made ☒ "as is" ☐ subject to the repairs, alterations, inspections or conditions listed below ☐ subject to completion per plans & specifications.

Conditions of Appraisal: Personal property items were not considered in the valuation of the real property.

Final Reconciliation: While the cost approach indicates a higher value, the sales comparison approach was given the in the final conclusion. As this type of property is typically owner-occupied, the income approach has ins

The purpose of this appraisal is to estimate the market value of the real property that is the subject of this report, based on the above conditions and the certification, contingent and limiting conditions, and market value definition that are stated in the attached Freddie Mac Form 439/FNMA form 1004B (Revised 6/93).

I (WE) ESTIMATE THE MARKET VALUE, AS DEFINED, OF THE REAL PROPERTY THAT IS THE SUBJECT OF THIS REPORT, AS OF June 2, 1998 (WHICH IS THE DATE OF INSPECTION AND THE EFFECTIVE DATE OF THIS REPORT) TO BE $ 429,000

APPRAISER:	SUPERVISORY APPRAISER (ONLY IF REQUIRED):	
Signature *Paul J. Piekos*	Signature	☐ Did ☐ Did Not
Name Paul J. Piekos SRA	Name	Inspect Property
Date Report Signed June 2, 1998	Date Report Signed	
State Certification # 156-XXXXXX State IL	State Certification # State	
Or State License # State	Or State License # State	

Freddie Mac Form 70 6/93   PAGE 2 OF 2   Fannie Mae Form 1004 6-93

Form UA2   "TOTAL 2000 for Windows" appraisal software by a la mode, inc.   1-800-ALAMODE

INDEPENDENT CONTRACTOR AGREEMENT

AGREEMENT made this <u>1st</u> day of <u> Feb </u>, 20<u>06</u> by and between <u>Real Estate Solutions, :</u> (hereinafter "Corporation") whose address is <u>Post Office Box 221, Denver, CO 80203</u> and <u>Carl Contractor</u> <u> </u>, whose address is <u> </u> <u>234 Havana St, Aurora, CO 80011</u> (hereinafter "Contractor").

SERVICES TO BE PERFORMED

Contractor agrees to perform the following services for Corporation:

<u>Repair drywall in kitchen and living room; paint bathroom</u>

PLACE OF PERFORMANCE

The work described above shall be performed at:<u> </u>
<u>123 Main Street, Denver, CO 80203</u>

TIME PERIOD

Contractor agrees to commence work as soon as practical and complete all work by <u>Feb 12th</u>, 20<u>06</u>. Contractor agrees to subtract $<u>50.00</u> per day for each day the work is not completed as liquidated damages and not as a penalty from the total bill of services performed.

PAYMENT FOR SERVICES

Contractor shall be paid not by the hour or the day, but upon complete of certain repairs as follows: <u>Upon completion of drywall 1/2 fee, balance after painting</u> completed

SUPERVISION

Corporation shall not supervise or directly control the work of Contractor. Corporation does reserve the right, from time to time, to inspect the work being performed to determine whether it is being performed in a good and "workmanlike" manner. Contractor shall have the ultimate authority to determine the hours of work, the length of workdays, the means and methods of performance of the work, and Corporation shall not interfere in this regard.

MATERIALS

Contractor will obtain and provide all necessary materials for the services described above at his own expense.

INVOICES

Contractor agrees to provide Corporation with written invoices for all work performed.

SUBCONTRACTORS OR ASSISTANTS

Contractor may, in his discretion and at his own expense, employ such assistants or subcontractors as may be necessary for the performance of work. Contractor agrees to pay any wages, taxes, unemployment insurance, withholding taxes, workers compensation insurance required by law for assistants or subcontractors. Said assistants or subcontractors will not be paid or supervised by Corporation.

EQUIPMENT

Contractor agrees to provide his own equipment or tools for the work to be performed.

INSURANCE

Contractor agrees to provide his own liability insurance for work performed, naming Corporation as additional insured. In the event that Contractor does not maintain insurance, he shall defend and indemnify Corporation for all lawsuits, accidents or claims arising out of his work, or the work of his assistants or
subcontractors.

INDEPENDENT CONTRACTOR

Contractor agrees that he is completely independent from Corporation and is not an employee of Corporation. Contractor warrants that he may, and in fact does work for other individuals and/or entities.

Carl Contractor
Contractor

Real Estate Solutions, Inc.
by Ira Investor, president
Corporation

JOINT VENTURE AGREEMENT

THIS JOINT VENTURE AGREEMENT (the "Agreement"), made and entered into as of this __1st__ day of ___Feb___, 20_06_ by and between __Real Estate Solutions, Inc.__ and __Anton Investor__ .

1. BUSINESS PURPOSE:

The business of the Joint Venture shall be to purchase certain real estate located at __123 Main Street, Denver, CO 80203__ in the County of ___Denver___, State of ___Colorado___ for the purpose of renovation and sale for profit.

2. TERM OF THE AGREEMENT:

This Joint Venture shall commence on the date first above written and shall continue in existence until terminated, liquidated, or dissolved by law or as hereinafter provided.

3. OBLIGATIONS OF THE JOINT VENTURERS:

[Set forth in detail the obligations of the parties, for example, who will contribute cash, property and other services, who will pay workers, who will supervise the project, who will contribute money for cost overruns, etc]

4. PROFITS AND LOSSES:

Upon the sale of the property and receipt of all proceeds therefrom, the parties will be reimbursed their actual, out of pocket expenses directed related to the Venture. After all expenses, debts and costs related to the Venture and the property, the parties agree to split the Net Proceeds as follows:

          __Anton Investor__ shall receive _50_ %

          __Real Estate Solutions, Inc__ shall receive _50_ %

5. <u>INDEMNIFICATION OF THE JOINT VENTURERS</u>:

The parties to this Agreement shall have no liability to the other for any loss suffered which arises out of any action or inaction if, in good faith, it is determined that such course of conduct was in the best interests of the Joint Venture and such course of conduct did not constitute negligence or misconduct. The parties to this Agreement shall each be indemnified by the other against losses, judgments, liabilities, expenses and amounts paid in settlement of any claims sustained by it in connection with the Joint Venture.

6. <u>DISSOLUTION</u>:

The Joint Venture shall be dissolved upon the happening of any of the following events:

(a) The adjudication of bankruptcy, filing of a petition pursuant to a Chapter of the Federal Bankruptcy Act, withdrawal, removal or insolvency of either of the parties.

(b) The sale or other disposition, not including an exchange of all, or substantially all, of the Joint Venture assets.

(c) Mutual agreement of the parties.

7. <u>COMPLETE AGREEMENT</u>:

This Agreement constitutes the full and complete understanding and agreement of the parties hereto with respect to the subject matter hereof, and there are no agreements, understandings, restrictions or warranties among the parties other than those set forth herein provided for.

8. <u>UNIFORM PARTNERSHIP ACT</u>

Anything not specifically set forth herein shall be governed by the applicable rules of the Uniform Partnership Act of the State of ___Colorado_____.

IN WITNESS WHEREOF, the parties hereto have executed this Agreement as of the day and year first above written. Signed, sealed and delivered in the presence of:

__Anton Investor_____
Joint Venturer

Real Estate Solutions, Inc.
by Ira Investor, president_____
Joint Venturer

D

STATE-BY-STATE FORECLOSURE GUIDE

The following is a summary of foreclosure laws and practices for all 50 states and the District of Columbia. This information is merely a summary and is not intended as a substitute for sound legal counsel.

The information is divided into five columns:

1. *State.* The state in which you are looking for foreclosure properties.
2. *Type of Security Most Commonly Used.* Although both deeds of trust and mortgages are available as collateral for a real estate loan, most lenders use one or the other exclusively in each state.
3. *Foreclosure Method.* The legal method by which the lender seeks to liquidate the collateral to recoup its funds.
4. *Redemption Period.* The amount of time, if any, a borrower has after the foreclosure sale date to come up with funds to keep the property.
5. *Misc.* Other information, such as a legal right for a borrower to reinstate the loan rather than pay it off in full.

State	Type of Security Most Commonly Used	Foreclosure Method	Redemption Period	Misc.
Alabama	Mortgage	Power of Sale	12 months	Borrower can reinstate his loan within 5 days of sale
Alaska	Deed of Trust	Power of Sale	None	Borrower can reinstate loan up to date of sale so long as a notice of default has not been filed more than 2 times in the past
Arizona	Deed of Trust	Power of Sale	None	
Arkansas	Deed of Trust	Power of Sale	Within one year	
California	Deed of Trust	Power of Sale	None	
Colorado	Deed of Trust	Power of Sale	75 days	Borrower can cure up to sale date
Connecticut	Mortgage	Strict Foreclosure	None, unless ordered by the court	A strict foreclosure vests title in the lender without a sale. Borrower cannot reinstate the loan. A court may delay the foreclosure for up to six months if the borrower is not making enough money!
Delaware	Mortgage	Judicial	None	
Dist. of Columbia	Deed of Trust	Power of Sale	None	Borrower can reinstate up to 45 days before sale once in two consecutive years
Florida	Mortgage	Judicial	Up to the date the clerk files the certificate of sale	
Georgia	Mortgage	Power of Sale	None	
Hawaii	Mortgage	Power of Sale	None	
Idaho	Deed of Trust	Power of Sale	None	Borrower can cure with-in 115 days of the filing of notice of default
Illinois	Mortgage	Judicial	Until the latter of 3 months of entry of judgment or 7 months of service of the foreclosure complaint	Borrower has 90 days from the service of the complaint to reinstate
Indiana	Mortgage	Judicial	None	
Iowa	Mortgage	Judicial	One year	

State	Type of Security Most Commonly Used	Foreclosure Method	Redemption Period	Misc.
Kansas	Mortgage	Judicial	3-12 months, depending on the property's equity	
Kentucky	Mortgage & Deed of Trust	Judicial	Up to one year if the sale does not bring at least ⅔ of the property's value	
Louisiana	Mortgage	Judicial	None	
Maine	Mortgage	Judicial	Within one year unless the mortgage agreement provides for less	Borrower can reinstate within 30 days of default
Maryland	Deed of Trust	Power of Sale with court supervision	None stated, although equitable redemption permitted	
Massachusetts	Mortgage	Power of Sale	None	
Michigan	Mortgage	Power of Sale	Varies, but generally 6 months on houses	
Minnesota	Mortgage	Power of Sale	6 to 12 months depending on equity	
Mississippi	Deed of Trust	Power of Sale	None	Borrower can reinstate up to the date of sale
Missouri	Deed of Trust	Power of Sale	One year if the lender purchases the property at sale	
Montana	Deed of Trust	Judicial	None	
Nebraska	Deed of Trust	Judicial	None	Borrower can reinstate before sale
Nevada	Deed of Trust	Power of Sale	None	Borrower has 35 days from filing of notice of default to reinstate loan
New Hampshire	Mortgage	Power of Sale	None	NH mortgage can also have a strict foreclosure provision
New Jersey	Mortgage	Judicial	6 months after entry of judgment	
New Mexico	Mortgage	Judicial	9 months, but may be as little as 1 month by agreement in writing	
New York	Mortgage	Judicial	None	
North Carolina	Deed of Trust	Power of Sale	None	

State	Type of Security Most Commonly Used	Foreclosure Method	Redemption Period	Misc.
North Dakota	Mortgage	Judicial	One year	
Ohio	Mortgage	Judicial	Only up to the date of confirmation of sale	
Oklahoma	Mortgage	Judicial	Only up to the date of confirmation of sale	
Oregon	Deed of Trust	Power of Sale	None	Borrower may reinstate up to 5 days before sale
Pennsylvania	Mortgage	Judicial	None	Borrower may reinstate before the sale, up to 3 times in one year
Rhode Island	Mortgage	Power of Sale	Up to 3 years by filing a lawsuit	
South Carolina	Mortgage	Judicial	None	
South Dakota	Mortgage	Power of Sale	None	Borrower can make lender go through a judicial foreclosure
Tennessee	Deed of Trust	Power of Sale	Up to 2 years	
Texas	Deed of Trust	Power of Sale	None	Borrower has 20 days from notice of default to reinstate loan
Utah	Deed of Trust	Judicial	6 months	Borrower can reinstate within 3 months of notice of default
Vermont	Mortgage	Strict Foreclosure	None	
Virginia	Deed of Trust	Power of Sale	None	
Washington	Deed of Trust	Power of Sale	None	Borrower can reinstate loan up to 11 days before sale
West Virginia	Deed of Trust	Power of Sale	None if the sale is confirmed by the court	Borrower has 10 days from notice of default to reinstate loan
Wisconsin	Mortgage	Judicial	None	Borrower has until sale date to cure default
Wyoming	Deed of Trust	Power of Sale	None	

E

INTERNET RESOURCES

Remodeling Sites

Plan your work. http://www.hometime.com
Remodel your house. http://www.diyonline.com
Super site. http://www.doityourself.com

Home Sale Information Online

Yahoo! Home Values. http://realestate.yahoo.com/re/homevalues
Dataquick. http://www.dataquick.com
First American Real Estate Services. http://www.firstamres.com

Foreclosure Listings

Foreclosures.com. http://www.foreclosures.com
Department of Housing and Urban Development. http://www.hud.gov

Fannie Mae. http://www.fanniemae.com/homes
Canadian Foreclosures. http://www.foreclosures.ca/realtors/
foreclosure_proceedings/index.lasso

Other Internet Real Estate Resources

Legalwiz.com. http://www.legalwiz.com—hosted by Attorney William Bronchick
Real Estate Convention. http://www.realestateconvention.com—annual real estate convention hosted by William Bronchick
Real Estate Investor Training. http://realestateinvestortraining.com—e-coaching program with William Bronchick
Creative Real Estate Online. http://www.creonline.com—gathering place for real estate investors
The Creative Investor. http://www.tcinvestor.com—member-based investor Web site
Dealmakers Online. http://www.dealmakerscafe.com–gathering place for real estate investors
Robert Bruss.com. http://www.robertbruss.com—Web site for syndicated real estate columnist Robert Bruss

abstract of title A compilation of the recorded documents relating to a parcel of land, from which an attorney may give an opinion as to the condition of title. Also known in some states as a *preliminary title report.*

acceleration A condition in a financing instrument giving the lender the power to declare all sums owed the lender immediately due and payable upon an event such as sale of the property. Also known as a *due-on-sale.*

acre An area that contains 43,560 square feet of land

acknowledgment A declaration made by a person signing a document before a notary public or other officer

adverse possession Most states have laws that permit someone to claim ownership of property that is occupied for a number of years. This is common where a fence is erected over a boundary line (called an *encroachment*) without the objection of the rightful owner. After a number of years, the person who erected the fence may be able to commence a court proceeding to claim ownership of the property.

agency A relationship in which the agent is given the authority to act on behalf of another person

all-inclusive deed of trust See *wraparound mortgage*

ALTA American Land Title Association

amortize To reduce a debt by regular payments of both principal and interest

appraised value The value of a property at a given time, based on facts regarding the location, improvements, etc., of the property and surroundings

appreciation An increase in the net value of real estate

appurtenance Anything attached to the land or used with it, passing to the new owner upon its sale

ARM An adjustable-rate mortgage; that is, a loan whose interest rate may adjust over time depending on certain factors or a pre-determined formula

arrears A payment that is made after it's due is in arrears. Interest is said to be paid in arrears because it is paid to the date of payment rather than in advance.

assignment of contract A process by which a person sells, transfers, and/or assigns rights under an agreement. Often used in the context of the assignment of a purchase contract by a buyer or the assignment of a lease by a tenant.

assumable loan A loan secured by a mortgage or deed of trust containing no due-on-sale provision. Most pre-1989 FHA loans and pre-1988 VA loans are assumable without qualification. Some newer loans may be assumed with the express permission of the note holder.

assumption of mortgage Agreement by a buyer to assume the liability under an existing note secured by a mortgage or deed of trust

attorney-in-fact An agency relationship in which a person holds a power of attorney allowing the execution of legal documents on behalf of another person

bankruptcy A provision of federal law whereby a debtor surrenders assets to the bankruptcy court and is relieved of the obligation to repay unsecured debts. After bankruptcy, the debtor is discharged and unsecured creditors may not pursue further collection efforts against the debtor. Secured creditors continue to be secured by property but may not take other action to collect.

balloon mortgage A note calling for periodic payments that are insufficient to fully amortize the face amount of a note prior to maturity so that a principal sum known as a *balloon* is due at maturity

basis The financial interest one has in a property for tax purposes. Basis is adjusted down by depreciation and up by capital improvements.

beneficiary One for whose benefit trust property is held. Also known as the *lender under a deed of trust.*

binder A report issued by a title insurance company setting forth the condition of title and setting forth conditions that, if satisfied, will cause a policy of title insurance to be issued. Also known as a *title commitment.*

building restriction line A required set-back a certain distance from the road within which no building may take place. This restriction may appear in the original subdivision plat, in restrictive covenants, or in building codes and zoning ordinances.

buyer's agent A real estate broker or agent who represents the buyer's interests, though typically the fee is a split of the listing broker's commission. Also known as the *selling agent.*

capital gain Profit from the sale of a capital asset, such as real property. A long-term capital gain is a gain derived from property held more than 12 months. Long-term gains can be taxed at lower rates than short-term gains.

caveat emptor Buyer beware. A seller is under no obligation to disclose defects but may not actively conceal a known defect or lie if asked.

certificate of occupancy A certificate issued by a local governmental body stating that a building may be occupied

chain of title The chronological order of conveyance of a parcel of land from the original owner to the present owner

closing The passing of a deed or mortgage, signifying the end of a sale or mortgage of real property. Also known in some areas as *passing papers* or *closing of escrow.*

closing costs Expenses incurred in the closing of a real estate or mortgage transaction. Most fees are associated with the buyer or borrower's loan. Closing costs typically include an origination fee, discount points, appraisal fee, title search and insurance, survey, taxes, deed recording fee, credit report, and notary fees.

cloud on title An uncertainty, doubt, or claim against the rights of the owner of a property, such as a recorded purchase contract or option

collateral Property that is pledged to secure a loan

commitment A written promise to make or insure a loan for a specified amount and on specified items. Also used in the context of title insurance (*title commitment*).

community property In community property states (Arizona, California, Idaho, Louisiana, Nevada, New Mexico, Texas, Washington, and Wisconsin), all property of husband and wife acquired after the marriage is presumed to belong to both, regardless of how it is titled.

comparables Properties used as comparisons to determine the value of a specified property

condemnation A judicial proceeding through which a governmental body takes ownership of a private property for a public use

condominium A structure of two or more units, the interior spaces of which are individually owned. The common areas are owned as tenants in common by the condominium owners, and ownership is restricted by an association.

contingency The dependence on a stated event that must occur before a contract is binding. Used both in the context of a loan and a contract of sale.

contract A legally enforceable agreement between two or more parties

contract of sale A bilateral (two-way) agreement wherein the seller agrees to sell and the buyer agrees to buy a certain parcel of land, usually with improvements. Also used to reference an *installment land contract.*

contract for deed. See *installment land contract*

conventional mortgage A loan neither insured by the FHA nor guaranteed by the VA

cooperative apartment A cooperative is a corporation that holds title to the land and building. Each co-op owner has shares of stock in the corporation that correspond to an equivalent proprietary lease of an apartment space. Co-ops were popular in New York City at one time but are less common now because of their lack of marketability due to high association fees.

counteroffer A rejection of a seller's offer, usually with an amended agreement to sell the property to the potential buyer on different terms from the original offer

credit report A report documenting the credit history and current status of a person's credit

deficiency The difference between the amount owed to a note holder and the proceeds received from a foreclosure sale. The lender may, in some states, obtain a *deficiency judgment* against the borrower for the difference.

delivery The transfer of a deed to the grantee so that the grantor may not revoke it. A deed, signed but held by the grantor, does not pass title.

depreciation Decrease in value to real property improvements caused by deterioration or obsolescence

documentary tax stamps Stamps affixed to a deed showing the amount of transfer tax. Some states simply charge the transfer tax without affixing stamps. Also known as *doc stamps*.

double closing A closing wherein a property is bought and then sold simultaneously. Also called *double escrow* and *flipping*.

due-on-sale clause A provision in a mortgage or deed of trust that gives the lender the option to require payment in full of the indebtedness on transfer of title to the property (or any interest therein)

earnest money A good faith deposit or down payment

easement An interest that one has in the land of another. May be created by grant, reservation, agreement, prescription, or necessary implication.

eminent domain A constitutional right for a governmental authority to acquire private property for public use by condemnation and the payment of just compensation

encroachment Construction or imposition of a structure onto the property of another

encumbrance A claim, lien, or charge against real property

equity The difference between the market value of the property and the homeowner's mortgage debt

equitable title The interest of the purchase under an installment land contract

escrow Delivery of a deed by a grantor to a third party for delivery to the grantee on the happening of a contingent event

escrow agent, escrow company Individual or company that performs closing services for real estate loans and sales transactions

escrow payment That portion of a borrower's monthly payment held in trust by the lender to pay for taxes, mortgage insurance, hazard insurance, lease payments, and other items as they become due. Also known as *impounds*.

estate From the English feudal system, this word defines the extent of one's ownership in a property

estate for years An estate limited to a term of years. An estate for years is commonly called a *lease*. On the expiration of the estate for years, the property reverts back to the former owner.

fee simple The highest form of ownership. An estate under which the owner is entitled to unrestricted powers to dispose of the property, which can be left by will or inherited. Also known as *fee* or *fee simple absolute*.

Federal Housing Administration (FHA) A federal agency that insures first mortgages, enabling lenders to lend a high percentage of the sale price

fixture An item of personal property attached to real property

Freddie Mac; Federal Home Loan Mortgage Corporation (FHLMC) A federal agency purchasing first mortgages, both conventional and federally insured, from members of the Federal Reserve System and the Federal Home Loan Bank System

foreclosure A proceeding to extinguish all rights, title, and interests of the owner(s) of property in order to sell the property to satisfy a lien against it. About half of the states use a mortgage foreclosure, which is a lawsuit in court. About half use a power of sale proceeding, which is dictated by a deed of trust and is usually less time-consuming than a foreclosure.

Ginnie Mae; Government National Mortgage Association (GNMA) A federal association working with FHA that offers special assistance in obtaining mortgages and purchases mortgages in a secondary capacity

good faith estimate A lender's estimate of closing costs and monthly payment required by RESPA

grant deed A deed commonly used in California to convey title. By law, a grant deed gives certain warranties of title.

grantee A person receiving an interest in a property

grantor A person granting or giving up an interest in a property

grantor/grantee index The most common document recording indexing system is by grantor (the person conveying an interest, usually the seller or mortgagor) and grantee (the person receiving an interest, usually the buyer or mortgagee). All documents conveying property or an interest therein (deed, mortgage, lease, easement, etc.) are recorded by the grantor's last name in the grantor index. The same transaction is cross-indexed by the grantee's last name in the grantee index.

heirs and assigns Words usually found in a contract or deed that indicate that the obligations assumed or interest granted are binding upon or sure to benefit the heirs or assigns of the party

homeowners' association An association of people who own homes in a given area for the purpose of improving or maintaining the quality of the area. Also used in the context of a *condominium association*.

impound account. Account held by a lender for payment of taxes, insurance, or other payments. Also known as an *escrow account.*

installment land contract (ILC) The ILC is an agreement wherein the buyer makes payments in a manner similar to a mortgage. The buyer has equitable title. However, the seller holds legal title to the property until the contract is paid off. The buyer has equitable title and, for all intents and purposes, is the owner of the property. Also known as a *contract for deed* or *contract of sale.*

installment sale A sale that involves the seller receiving payments over time. The Internal Revenue Code contains specific definitions and promulgates specific rules concerning installment sales and tax treatment of them. Also known as an *owner carry* sale.

insured mortgage A mortgage insured against loss to the mortgagee in the event of default and failure of the mortgaged property to satisfy the balance owing plus costs of foreclosure

interest rate The percentage of an amount of money that is paid for its use for a specified time

joint and several liability A liability that allows a creditor to collect against any one of the debtors for the entire amount of the debt, regardless of fault or culpability. Most mortgage notes that are signed by husband and wife create joint and several liability.

joint tenancy An undivided interest in property, taken by two or more joint tenants. The interests must equal, accruing under the same conveyance and beginning at the same time. On death of a joint tenant, the interest passes to the surviving joint tenants rather than to the heirs of the deceased.

judgment The decision of a court of law. Money judgments, when recorded, become a lien on real property of the defendant.

junior mortgage Mortgage of lesser priority than the previously recorded mortgage

land lease Owners of property will sometimes give long-term leases of land up to 99 years. A lease of more than 99 years is considered a transfer of fee simple. Land leases are commonly used to build banks, car lots, and shopping malls.

land trust A revocable, living trust primarily used to hold title to real estate for privacy and anonymity. Also known as an *Illinois land trust* or *nominee trust.* The land trustee is a nominal *title holder,* with the beneficiaries having the exclusive right to direct and control the actions of the trustee.

lease/option An agreement by which the lessee (tenant) has the unilateral option to purchase the leased premises from the lessor (landlord). Some lease/option agreements provide for a portion of the rent to be applied toward the purchase price. The price may be fixed at the beginning of the agreement or be determined by another formula, such as an appraisal at a later time. Also referred to as a *lease/ purchase.*

lease/purchase Often used interchangeably with the expression *lease/ option,* but technically means a lease in conjunction with a bilateral purchase agreement. Often used by real estate agents to mean a purchase agreement whereby the tenant takes possession prior to close of escrow.

lien An encumbrance against property for money, either voluntary (e.g., mortgage), involuntary (e.g., judgment), or by operation of law (e.g., property tax lien)

life estate An estate in real property for the life of a living person. The estate then reverts back to the grantor or to a third party.

lis pendens A legal notice recorded to show pending litigation relating to real property and giving notice that anyone acquiring an interest in said property subsequent to the date of the notice may be bound by the outcome of the litigation. Often filed prior to a mortgage foreclosure proceeding.

license An authority to do a particular act or series of acts upon the land of another without possessing any estate or interest therein (e.g., a ski lift ticket). A license is similar to an easement in that it gives someone permission to cross property for a specific purpose. An easement is a property interest, whereas a license is a contractual right.

liquidated damages A contract clause that limits a party to a certain sum in lieu of actual damages. In the case of a real estate purchase and sale contract, the seller's legal remedy is limited to the buyer's earnest money deposit.

loan-to-value ratio The ratio of the mortgage loan amount to the property's appraised value (or the selling price, whichever is less)

market analysis A report estimating the resale value of a property. Usually prepared by a real estate agent showing comparable sales of properties in the vicinity based on tax records and information from the multiple listing service.

marketable title Title that can be readily marketed to a reasonably prudent purchaser aware of the facts and their legal meaning concerning liens and encumbrances

mechanic's lien A lien created by state law for the purpose of securing priority of payment for the price of value of work performed and materials furnished in construction or repair of improvements to land, and which attach to the land as well as the improvements

metes and bounds A method of describing land by directions and distances rather than reference to a lot number

mortgage A security instrument given by a borrower to secure performance of payment under a note. The document is recorded in county land records, creating a lien (encumbrance) on the property. Also known as a *deed of trust* in some states. The borrower is also called a *mortgagor.*

mortgage broker One who, for a fee, brings together a borrower and lender, and handles the necessary applications for the borrower to obtain a loan against real property by giving a mortgage or deed of trust as security

mortgagee A lender

mortgagor A borrower

Mortgage Guaranty Insurance Corporation (MGIC) A private corporation that, for a fee, insures mortgage loans similar to FHA and VA insurance, although not insuring as great a percentage of the loan

mortgage insurance Insurance required for loans with a loan-to-value ratio above 80 percent. Also called *PMI* or *MIP.*

multiple listing service A service performed by the Local Board of REALTORS® that provides information to aid in the sale of properties to a wide market base

notary public One authorized by law to acknowledge and certify documents and signatures as valid

note A written promise to repay a certain sum of money under specified terms. Also known as a *promissory note.*

offer A proposal to buy

option The unilateral right to do something. For example, the right to renew a lease or purchase a property. The optionee is the holder of the option. The optionor is the grantor of the option. The optionor is bound by the option, but the optionee is not.

origination fee A fee or charge for work involved in the evaluation, preparation, and submission of a proposed mortgage loan, usually about 1 percent of the loan amount

payoff amount A total amount of money needed to satisfy full payment on an existing loan or lien

performance mortgage A mortgage or deed of trust given to secure performance of an obligation other than a promissory note

periodic tenancy An estate from week-to-week, month-to-month, etc. In the absence of a written agreement (or on the expiration of a lease once payments are accepted), a periodic tenancy is created. Either party can terminate this type of arrangement by giving notice, usually equal to the amount of the period, or as prescribed by state law.

PITI Principal, interest, taxes, and insurance

plat A map showing the division of a piece of land

points Fee paid by a borrower to obtain a loan. A point is 1 percent of the principal amount of the loan. The borrower may pay more points to reduce the interest rate of the loan.

power of attorney A written document authorizing another to act on one's behalf as an attorney in fact

prepayment penalty An additional charge imposed by the lender for paying off a loan before its due date

probate A court process to prove a will is valid

promissory note A written, unsecured note promising to pay a specified amount of money on demand, often transferable to a third party

prorate To divide in proportionate shares. Used in the context of a closing, at which such things as property taxes, interest, rents, and other items are adjusted in favor of the seller, buyer, or lender.

purchase agreement A binding agreement between parties for the purchase of real estate

purchase-money mortgage A loan obtained in conjunction with the purchase of real estate

quiet title proceeding A court action to establish or clear up uncertainty as to ownership of real property. Often required if a lien or cloud appears on a title that cannot be resolved.

quitclaim deed A deed by which the grantor gives up any claim he or she may have in the property. Often used to clear up a cloud on a title.

real estate Land and anything permanently affixed to the land and those things attached to the buildings

real property Land and whatever by nature or artificial annexation is attached to it.

REALTOR® Any member of the National Association of Realtors

recording The act of publicly filing a document, such as a deed or mortgage

recourse note A note under which the holder can look to the borrower's personal assets for payment

redemption The right, in some states, for an owner or lien holder to satisfy the indebtedness due on a mortgage in foreclosure after sale

refinancing The repayment of a loan from the proceeds of a new loan using the same property as collateral

reissue rate A discounted charge for a title insurance policy if a previous policy on the same property was issued within a specified period (usually three to five years)

release An instrument releasing a lien or encumbrance (e.g., mortgage) from a property

RESPA (Real Estate Settlement Procedures Act) A federal law requiring disclosure of certain costs in the sale of residential property that is to be financed by a federally insured lender. Also requires that the lender provide a good faith estimate of closing costs prior to closing of the loan.

second mortgage A loan secured by a mortgage or trust deed, of which lien is junior to a first mortgage or deed of trust

secondary mortgage market The buying and selling of first mortgages and deeds of trust by banks, insurance companies, government agencies, and other mortgagees

security instrument A document under which collateral is pledged (e.g., mortgage)

settlement statement A statement prepared by a closing agent (usually a title or escrow company) giving a complete breakdown of costs and charges involved in a real estate transaction. Required by RESPA on a form HUD-1.

special assessment Tax imposed by the local government for public improvements, such as new streets

special warranty deed A seller warrants he or she has done nothing to impair title but makes no warranty prior to his or her ownership

specific performance An action to compel the performance of a contract

subdivision Division of land into lots and streets, typically under strict requirements of the state and county

sublet To let or lease part of one's estate in a lease. A subtenant is not in privity of contract with the landlord and neither can look to each other for performance of a lease agreement.

subject to When transferring title to a property encumbered by a mortgage lien without paying off the debt or assuming the note, the buyer is taking title "subject to."

subordination The process by which a lien holder agrees to permit a lien to become junior or subordinate to another lien

tenancy in common With tenancy in common, each owner (called a *tenant*) has an undivided interest in the possession of the property. Each tenant's interest is salable and transferable. Each tenant can convey that interest by deed, mortgage, or will. Joint ownership is presumed to be in common if nothing further is stated on the deed.

tenancy by the entirety A form of ownership recognized in some states by which husband and wife each owns the entire property. As with joint tenancy, in event of death of one, the survivor owns the property without probate. In some states, tenancy by entirety protects the property from obligations of one spouse.

testate When a person dies with a will

title Title is the evidence of ownership. In essence, title is more important than ownership, because having proper title is proof of ownership. If you have a problem with your title, you will have trouble proving your ownership and thus selling or mortgaging your property.

title insurance An insurance policy that protects the insured (purchaser and/or lender) against loss arising from defects in title. A policy protecting the lender is called a *loan policy,* whereas a policy protecting the purchaser is called an *owner's policy.* Virtually all transactions involving a loan require title insurance.

title search An examination of the public records to disclose facts concerning the ownership of real estate

truth in lending Federal law requiring, among other things, a disclosure of interest rate charges and other information about a loan

trust A right to or in property held for the benefit of another, which may be written or implied

trustee One who holds property in trust for another party

trustor One who creates a trust by granting property to a trustee. Also known as the *borrower* on a deed of trust

VA loan A long-term, low or no down payment loan guaranteed by the Department of Veterans Affairs, which is offered to individuals qualified by military service or other entitlements

warranty deed A deed under which the seller makes a guarantee or warranty that the title is marketable and that the seller will defend all claims against it

wraparound mortgage A mortgage that is subordinate to and incorporates the terms of an underlying mortgage. The mortgagor (borrower) makes payments to the mortgagee (lender), who then makes payments on an underlying mortgage. Also referred to as an *all-inclusive deed of trust* in some states.

yield spread premium A kickback from the lender to the mortgage broker for the additional profit made from marking up the interest rate on a loan

zoning Regulation of private land use and development by a local government

Index

Share the message!

Bulk discounts
Discounts start at only 10 copies and range from 30% to 55% off retail price based on quantity.

Custom publishing
Private label a cover with your organization's name and logo. Or, tailor information to your needs with a custom pamphlet that highlights specific chapters.

Ancillaries
Workshop outlines, videos, and other products are available on select titles.

Dynamic speakers
Engaging authors are available to share their expertise and insight at your event.

Call Kaplan Publishing Corporate Sales at
1-800-621-9621, ext. 4444,
or e-mail kaplanpubsales@kaplan.com